Hip Grooves for Hand Drums

How to Play Funk, Rock, & World-Beat Patterns On Any Drum

by Alan Dworsky and Betsy Sansby

Cover art by Toni Pawlowsky

Instructional illustrations by Jay Kendell

Patterns on the CD played by Marc Anderson

DANCING HANDS MUSIC

Hip Grooves for Hand Drums – How to Play Funk, Rock,
& World-Beat Patterns on Any Drum

Published by
Dancing Hands Music
4275 Churchill Circle
Minnetonka, MN, 55345
phone or fax: 952-933-0781
dancinghands.com

Book design and layout by MacLean & Tuminelly
Cover art by Toni Pawlowsky
Illustrations by Jay Kendell except for the illustration on page 83 by
Robert Jackson

Patterns on the CD played by Marc Anderson, marcanderson.com

Printed in the United States of America
with soy ink on recycled, acid-free paper by Banta ISG (Viking Press)

ISBN 0-9638801-5-2

To Barb and Jim,
our best friends

Table of Contents

CHAPTER 1

Who this book is for and how it works

You don't need a drumset to lay down a groove. All you need is one drum. It can be a djembe, a conga, or anything else you can get both your hands on. Whether your goal is to play in a band, jam in the park, or just drum along with your favorite CDs, this book will show you how, step by step.

There are no boring exercises in this book, just great dance grooves. Many of them are adapted from drumset patterns used in rock, pop, and funk music. Others are based on traditional African or Afro-Cuban rhythms. You can play all these grooves in a wide variety of musical styles and settings. And you can hear how each one sounds on the CD that comes with the book.

If you've never played a hand drum before, that's okay. We'll show you how to make all the basic strokes on a djembe or a conga in the very first lesson. These same techniques can be applied to almost any hand drum. We use life-like illustrations to show how each stroke looks from the outside and give detailed descriptions to explain how each stroke feels from the inside.

If you've never read music before, that's okay too. We use simple box charts that even non-musicians find easy to understand. And we don't just dump a pile of charts on you and split. We'll be with you every step of the way, anticipating your questions, pointing out whatever is most important, and explaining whatever we think will make your journey easier.

The book is organized into eleven lessons arranged roughly in order of difficulty. Within each lesson, the patterns start simple and gradually get more complex. But you'll hardly notice it, because we make sure you get the right-size steps, in the right order, at just the right time.

We've done everything else we could to make this book as user-friendly as possible. Whenever we introduce a new Playing Principle or Practice Principle, we highlight it in the margin for easy reference. Whenever we introduce a new term, we print it in bold letters, define it on the spot, and toss it in the Glossary. Whenever we introduce a new musical concept, we separate it and explain it in a Musical Time Out. At the back of the book you'll find blank charts you can photocopy and use for writing down new patterns. And on the CD we've recorded one pattern from every lesson for a full two minutes so you can play along.

On the next page, we explain how to read the charts and work with the CD. After that, we get right down to business. So turn off the ringer on your phone, grab your drum, and let's get started.

CHAPTER 2

How to read the charts and work with the CD

Here's a sample chart:

PATTERN 1-6

1	+	2	+	3	+	4	+	1	+	2	+	3	+	4	+
✳	•	•	•	Δ	•	•	•	✳	•	•	•	Δ	•	•	•
R	L	R	L	R	L	R	L	R	L	R	L	R	L	R	L

Box charts like these are the simplest charts for notating drum rhythms. Time moves from left to right and each vertical column shows what's happening on a single beat. Each of the three horizontal rows gives you a different kind of information.

The top row – or "count row" – tells you how to count a rhythm. The symbol "+" stands for "AND." The shaded boxes on the count row indicate the pulse, which we'll explain in Lesson 1.

The middle row tells you when and how to hit the drum. If there's a symbol in a box, you hit the drum on that beat with the stroke indicated by the symbol. For example, in the chart above, there's an asterisk in the box under beat 1. The asterisk is the symbol for the bass stroke, so you play a bass stroke on beat 1.

Here are all the symbols for how to hit the drum:

Bass tone	=	✳
Open tone	=	O
Slap	=	▲
Touch or toe stroke	=	•
Heel stroke	=	◡
Drop stroke	=	◡̇

The bottom row on the chart tells you which hand to use. Although you'll be using both hands on all the patterns, most of them start with the right hand. If you're left-handed, you can reverse the hands.

To make the charts as big as possible, we've made them just long enough to show a single repetition of each pattern. But you should think of every chart as being written in a circle. When you get to the end, go back to the beginning and start over without missing a beat.

Think of every chart as being written in a circle. When you get to the end, go back to the beginning and start over without missing a beat.

We haven't put any tempo markings on our charts. Ultimately, the tempo of a rhythm will depend on your playing situation. The important thing for now is to play each pattern at a steady tempo and not to leave a pattern until it grooves.

This system of notation works great for teaching you the patterns in this book. But no system of written notation can capture the subtle nuances of a live rhythm. So while you're working your way through this book, be sure to listen to how the patterns are played on the CD.

Each track on the CD corresponds to the lesson with the same number. The first thing you'll hear on each track is one of the patterns from that lesson played up to speed. Don't worry about trying to learn it yet. Just listen and enjoy. It's only intended as an introduction to give you a feel for how the patterns in that lesson can sound once you've mastered them.

Immediately following the introductory pattern, you'll hear each pattern in the lesson introduced by number and played slowly for several repetitions. We recommend that before you try playing a pattern you listen to it on the CD. Knowing how a pattern is supposed to sound will help you play it correctly.

Finally, at the end of each track you'll hear the same pattern you heard at the start of the track, only this time you'll hear it played at a moderate tempo for a full two minutes so you can play along. You'll know which pattern in each lesson is the play-along pattern by the following label above the chart: PLAY-ALONG

That's all you need to know for now. We'll explain everything else as we go along.

CHAPTER 3

Playing Position

Most hand drums can be played either standing up or sitting down. Standing up gives you more mobility and visibility, which may be important if you're performing. But sitting down gives you more stability. So if you're new to hand drums, we recommend you play sitting down at first. That way all your energy and focus can go into mastering the basic strokes and the rhythms. Playing standing up is a separate skill that takes time and practice to master.

To play sitting down, the first thing you need is a good chair. It should be sturdy enough to provide a solid foundation for you while you play. A typical kitchen chair will work, but if you're shorter or taller than average you may need to find a chair of a different height. When you're sitting at the right height, your thighs will be parallel to the floor when your feet are flat on the floor.

Find a chair without arms or you'll end up bumping your elbows on them while you play. And the chair should be open in front so when you tilt the drum you can slide the bottom a little ways under the seat.

Once you've got your chair, sit towards the front of it. If you've got a drum that rests on the floor, tilt it forward away from your body – just like the drummer on the back cover is doing. The angle of the drumhead in relation to the floor should be somewhere between 10 and 45 degrees.

Tilting the drum allows the sound to come out the bottom. The further you tilt it forward, the more the sound comes out – especially the bass. Tilting the drum also brings your hands and arms into proper alignment with the drumhead so your wrists aren't cramped and your hands and arms can move freely.

If you're playing on carpet, you may want to put a piece of plywood under the drum so the carpet doesn't muffle the sound. On the other hand, if you need to play quietly, playing on carpet is a good idea.

Once you're comfortable holding your drum in a tilted position, place your hands on the drumhead in this position:

If you think of the drumhead as the face of an old-fashioned clock, your right hand should be between the 4 and 5 and your left hand between the 7 and 8. Keep your hands in line with your forearms, so that you could draw a straight line from your elbow through your middle finger. Consider this hand position home base.

If you're playing a djembe, look at the drumhead to see if there's a line across the middle. If there is, that's the spine of the goatskin. Turn the drum so that this line points straight at you. This is usually the best position for getting an even sound in both hands. If there are irregularities around the edge of your drumhead that might hurt your hands, try rotating the drum 180 degrees.

Before you start playing, always take off any rings you're wearing. These can hurt your hands and damage the drumhead. You should also take off your watch or any bracelets that might touch the drumhead or rattle while you play. If the cuff of your shirt is loose, roll it up and make sure it stays out of the way too.

Finally, check your posture. Your spine should be straight, you should be leaning slightly forward from the waist, your shoulders should be down and relaxed, and your elbows should be hanging loosely at your sides.

Now you're ready to play.

CHAPTER 4

The Patterns

lesson **1**

Slap on the backbeat in four

By the time you finish this lesson, you'll be able to play a dance groove that will fit with most popular music. And while you're learning it, you'll also be learning how to make all the basic strokes. We recommend that you read through the instruction on technique even if you've been playing for a while. Each stroke is explained in great detail, so you're bound to learn something new.

The three main strokes on any hand drum are the bass, the tone, and the slap. We start with the bass because it's the easiest. Depending on your drum, the bass stroke will produce a resonant boom or a dull thud. This sound is the hand-drum equivalent of the sound produced by the bass drum in a drumset.

To make a bass stroke, move your hand up and forward from the home base position toward the center of the drum, along the imaginary line running through your forearm and middle finger. Then simply bring it down onto the center of the drum and let it bounce up. Keep your fingers relaxed and together. Your thumb can be either pulled in against your index finger or extended away from your hand:

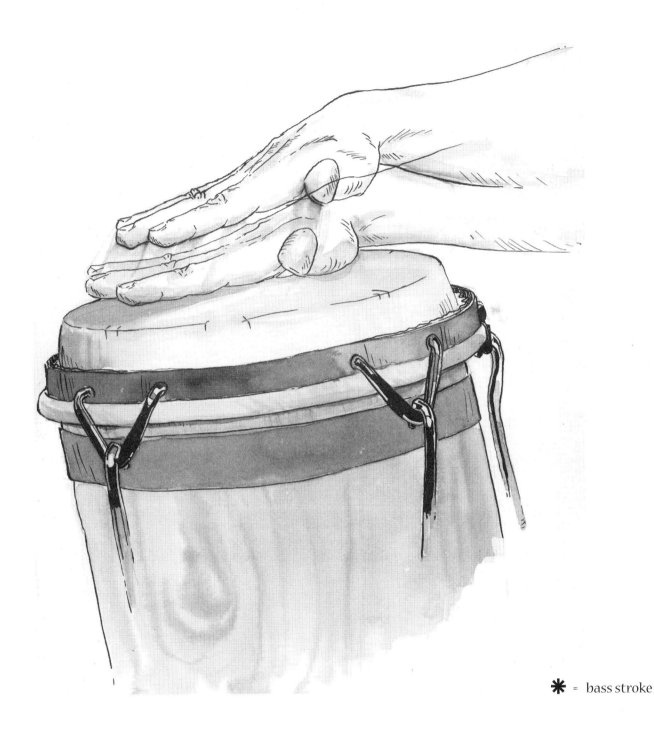

✳ = bass stroke

Most of the sound of the bass stroke comes from your palm, so that's where you should focus the weight of your hand. You can also let your fingers make contact with the drumhead by keeping your whole hand flat, or you can lift your fingers slightly so only the palm makes contact. Experiment to see what sounds best on your drum and feels best to you.

Once you're comfortable playing bass strokes with both hands, you're ready to play them in time. Start by counting out loud "1 AND 2 AND 3 AND 4 AND." Then keep counting and play bass strokes on beats 1 and 3 with alternating hands. Remember to think of this chart – and every chart – as being written in a circle. When you get to the end, go right back to the beginning and start over without missing a beat:

PATTERN 1-1

1	+	2	+	3	+	4	+	1	+	2	+	3	+	4	+
✻				✻				✻				✻			
R				L				R				L			

You've just played the pulse in four. The **pulse** is the underlying metronomic rhythm people feel in their bodies when music is played. When you tap your foot to music, chances are you're tapping along with the pulse. When you dance, chances are you're moving your feet to the pulse.

Since all the patterns in this book are dance grooves, they're all organized around a pulse. You should know where the pulse is in whatever pattern you're playing at all times. That's why we recommend you get in the habit of keeping a pulse going in your body while you play. One way is to tap your foot. If that's not easy to do while holding your drum, find somewhere else in your body to put the pulse: nod your head, move your shoulders, rock your midsection or your pelvis. The idea is to express your internal awareness of the pulse as an external body movement.

PLAYING
PRINCIPLE

Keep a pulse going
in your body while
you play.

To help you keep track of the pulse, we shade it on the count row of every chart. In four, the way we're counting, the pulse falls on 1 and 3 in each measure. That's why those boxes are shaded on the chart above.

Musical Time-Out: Counting in four

When we say a pattern is in **four**, we mean it can be notated on a chart with four pulses and four subdivisions – or **beats** – to each pulse. Our charts in four are divided into two measures of eighth-note beats. The pulse falls on beats 1 and 3 in each measure. This way of counting is called **cut-time**:

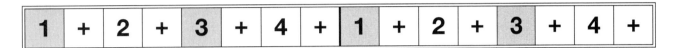

We could have counted patterns in four in **4/4 time**. In 4/4, a measure is divided into four quarter notes, and each quarter note is divided into four sixteenth notes. This way of counting has the advantage of putting the pulse on each numbered beat:

It's best to know how to count both ways. But since we had to make a choice we chose to chart in cut-time rather than 4/4 for several reasons. We find it's easier to work with two short 8-beat measures than with one long 16-beat measure. We also like the counting system in cut-time better because it gives you a number as a reference point every two beats instead of every four. And we find it easier and more natural to talk about rhythms in cut-time. We'd feel silly talking about the "ee" of 3 or the "uh" of 4.

If you're used to counting in 4/4 and don't want to change, you don't have to. Just think of each eighth note on our charts as a sixteenth note instead. This won't change the sound or the speed of the patterns. And to help you out, we've included a chart in 4/4 for at least one of the patterns in each lesson.

Now you're ready to learn your second stroke: the open tone or "tone" for short. Of the three basic strokes, the tone is in the middle register between the bass on the low end and the slap on top. Depending on the drum, the tone can sound dry and muted or round and bright.

When you make an open tone, the alignment of your hand in relation to the edge of the drumhead is critical. Your hand should make contact with the edge of the drumhead at the crease where your fingers join the palm:

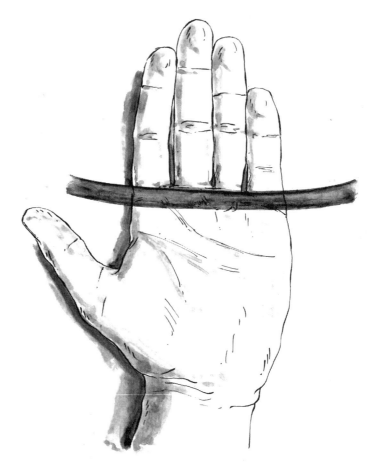

The easiest way to get the feel of the open tone stroke is to pretend you're dribbling a basketball. Raise your fingers a few inches off the drum by flexing your wrist and lifting your forearm slightly. Keep your fingers relaxed and together or slightly apart, and keep your thumb extended away from your hand so you don't whack it on the edge of the drum.

Now bring your hand down and bounce your fingers off the drumhead. The part of your palm just below the crease where your fingers join the hand should make only light contact with the edge of the drum. Don't let your fingers linger on the drumhead or you'll muffle the tone:

O = open tone

Now that you understand the basic hand-position and motion required to make an open tone, we want to focus on some details about the stroke that you can't pick up by watching someone play. When you make an open tone, your fingers should make contact with the drumhead between the crease where the fingers join the palm and the last knuckle of each finger. The pads of your fingertips – the fingerprint zone – should touch the drumhead just barely or not at all. And the weight of your hand should be focused as much as possible on the bony joint at the first knuckle away from the palm:

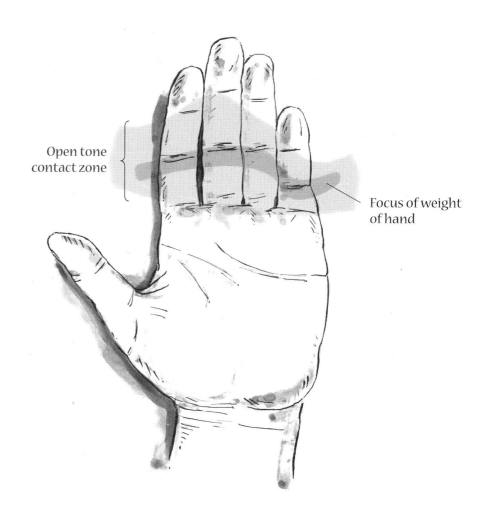

Open tone
contact zone

Focus of weight
of hand

Once you've played an open tone, if you don't need to make another
stroke immediately with the same hand, you can let your wrist drop
and leave your hand resting on the edge of the drum. You can also let
your thumb drop down below the edge of the drum if you want. Just
make sure your fingers are up so they don't muffle the head.

Now play open tones on the pulse with alternating hands. Count out
loud at first while you play:

PATTERN 1-2

1	+	2	+	3	+	4	+	1	+	2	+	3	+	4	+
O				O				O				O			
R				L				R				L			

Now that you know how to make two strokes, you're ready to put them together in a simple pattern using just your right hand. You'll still be playing the pulse, but this time you'll alternate between a bass on 1 and a tone on 3. Notice how this simple change makes a dramatic difference in how the pulse sounds:

PATTERN 1-3

1	+	2	+	3	+	4	+	1	+	2	+	3	+	4	+
✳				O				✳				O			
R				R				R				R			

The tones in this pattern fall on the **backbeats**, which we define as every second pulse in a pattern with two or four pulses. In four – the way we're counting – every second pulse falls on beat 3 in each measure. In 4/4, the backbeats fall on 2 and 4:

PATTERN 1-3:

1	e	+	a	2	e	+	a	3	e	+	a	4	e	+	a
✳				O				✳				O			
R				R				R				R			

From rock to pop to funk to hip-hop, the backbeat is the backbone of most dance music. On a drumset, the backbeat is usually played on a snare drum using a technique called a rimshot, which produces a loud crack. On a hand drum, the closest thing to a rimshot is a slap, so that's what you're going to be using for your backbeats.

But before we explain how to make the slap we need to warn you. Of the three basic strokes, the slap is the most difficult to master and the hardest on your hands. So please, go easy at first. Don't hurt yourself by hitting the drum too hard too soon.

Now let's look at the slap. It's produced by bringing your fingertips down onto the drumhead with a whip-like motion. Only the pad of each fingertip – the fingerprint section – should make contact with the drumhead:

PLAYING PRINCIPLE

The backbeat is the backbone of most dance music.

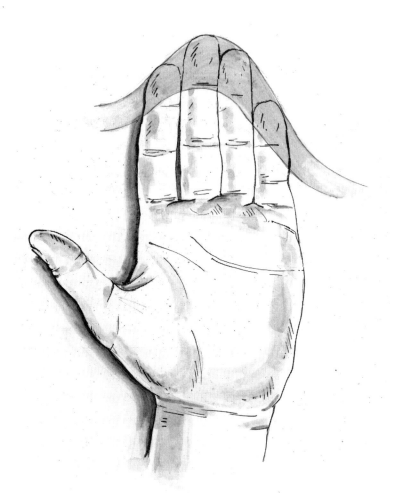

As with the open tone, the relation of your palm to the edge of the drum is critical. Starting from the open tone position, move your hand an inch or two forward toward the center of the drum, until the chubby part of your palm is resting on the edge. This is where your palm should make contact with the drum when you make a slap:

Next we want you to try an exercise that will help you get the feel of a slap stroke before you try the real thing. Rest the chubby part of your palm on the edge of the drum with your fingers raised, relaxed, and slightly curved. Now – without lifting your palm – bring your fingers down onto the drumhead. Make sure you make contact with just the fingerprint section of each finger. Do this exercise with alternating hands until the motion feels comfortable.

Now for the real thing. Start by lifting your hand two or three inches off the drum by raising your forearm slightly. At the same time, flex your wrist and pull your fingers up until your hand makes at least a 45 degree angle with the drumhead. Keep your fingers relaxed and together or slightly apart. Your thumb should be away from your hand, but it can be closer than when you made the open tone, because once you move your hand forward you don't need to worry about whacking your thumb on the rim.

Now throw your fingers down onto the drumhead in a whip-like motion while you bring the chubby part of your palm into light contact with the edge of the drum. It may help to imagine that the pad of each fingertip is a lead weight and the rest of each finger is completely weightless. When the pads of your fingertips make contact with the drumhead you have two choices. You can hold them down on the head for a moment with a slight gripping motion. This is called a **closed slap**, and it's used by conga drummers:

Or you can bounce your fingers off the drumhead immediately. This is called an **open slap** and it's used by both conga drummers and djembe players:

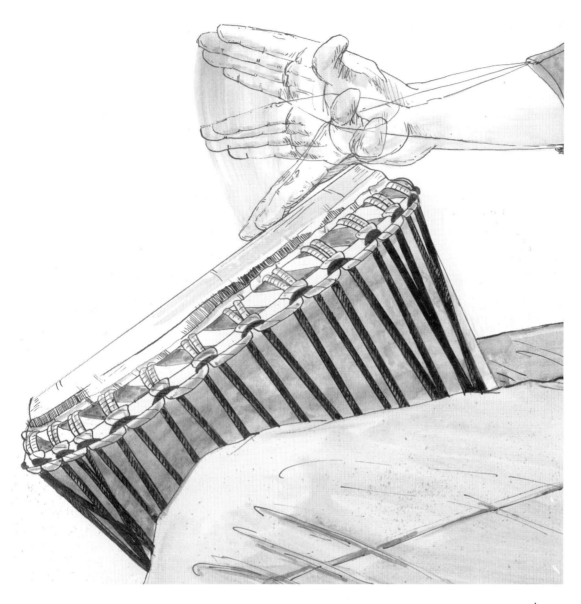

Now play slaps on the pulse with alternating hands. Try playing both closed and open slaps:

Δ = slap

PATTERN 1-4

1	+	2	+	3	+	4	+	1	+	2	+	3	+	4	+
Δ				Δ				Δ				Δ			
R				L				R				L			

You can turn this simple pattern into an exercise in self-awareness by paying attention to each slap you make. When you get a slap that sounds good and feels comfortable, stop and analyze what you just did. Ask yourself: "What was different that time?" "What made that one better than the rest?" You might find that you get a better sound by centering the force of the slap on a particular finger or fingers. Since everyone's hands are different, ultimately your own body will be your best teacher.

Since everyone's hands are different, ultimately your own body will be your best teacher.

As you practice, remember that the sound of the slap comes not from sheer force but from a relaxed snap of the wrist. If your hands hurt, you're doing something wrong. So only play as loud as you can play comfortably. As your technique improves, you'll be able to play louder with less effort.

Now you're ready to play slaps on the backbeat. The next pattern is the same as pattern 1-3, only with slaps in place of the open tones:

PATTERN 1-5

1	+	2	+	3	+	4	+	1	+	2	+	3	+	4	+
✻				Δ				✻				Δ			
R				R				R				R			

Next you're going to add touches to the pattern you just played. Touches are just what their name implies: light, relaxed strokes played with the pads of your fingertips. They should be played quietly so they add texture to a groove without obscuring or competing with the main strokes.

Touches can also help you keep steady time. When you fill in every empty beat in a pattern with touches, your hands become your metronome.

When you fill in every empty beat in a pattern with touches, your hands become your metronome.

We use touches in all the patterns in this book. That's because we want you to be able to carry a groove all by yourself. Touches help you do that by making the patterns you play sound more full. In traditional African and Afro-Cuban ensembles, you don't need all those touches because there are other drummers playing other parts to fill out the rhythm. In that context, adding touches would only add clutter.

Now you're going to fill in the empty beats in the pattern you just played with touches. Remember to play them significantly softer than the basses and slaps. Be sure to listen to the pattern on the CD to hear the difference in volume between the main strokes on the pulse and the touches:

• = touch

PATTERN 1-6

1	+	2	+	3	+	4	+	1	+	2	+	3	+	4	+
✳	•	•	•	Δ	•	•	•	✳	•	•	•	Δ	•	•	•
R	L	R	L	R	L	R	L	R	L	R	L	R	L	R	L

There you have it: the dance groove we promised you. It's simple but elegant, and it goes with almost everything. You may recognize it as a popular drumset pattern. In this adaptation for the hand drum, the bass strokes mimic the bass drum, the slaps mimic the snare, and the touches mimic the hi-hat. Here's the pattern charted in 4/4:

PATTERN 1-6 (IN 4/4)

1	e	+	a	2	e	+	a	3	e	+	a	4	e	+	a
✳	•	•	•	Δ	•	•	•	✳	•	•	•	Δ	•	•	•
R	L	R	L	R	L	R	L	R	L	R	L	R	L	R	L

Now you're ready to play a few variations. Start by replacing the touch on the AND of 3 in the first measure (we've gone back to counting in cut-time) with a slap in the left hand. Notice how adding the extra slap in the first measure creates a feeling of openness – like a comma in a sentence – while the single slap on the backbeat in the second measure creates a feeling of closure – like a period:

PATTERN 1-7

1	+	2	+	3	+	4	+	1	+	2	+	3	+	4	+
✳	•	•	•	Δ	Δ	•	•	✳	•	•	•	Δ	•	•	•
R	L	R	L	R	L	R	L	R	L	R	L	R	L	R	L

When you reverse the order of the two measures, the feeling of openness moves to the second measure:

PATTERN 1-8

1	+	2	+	3	+	4	+	1	+	2	+	3	+	4	+
✳	•	•	•	Δ	•	•	•	✳	•	•	•	Δ	Δ	•	•
R	L	R	L	R	L	R	L	R	L	R	L	R	L	R	L

The next pattern is the same as the last, except we've filled in the last two beats with tones. This creates a **fill** – a rhythmic bridge between repetitions of a pattern or sections of a song. When you play the fill – moving from slaps to tones and back to the bass on 1 – the falling pitches create a cascading sound. Drumset players do the same thing by moving from the snare to a tom to the bass drum.

PATTERN 1-9   PLAY-ALONG

1	+	2	+	3	+	4	+	1	+	2	+	3	+	4	+
✳	•	•	•	Δ	•	•	•	✳	•	•	•	Δ	Δ	O	O
R	L	R	L	R	L	R	L	R	L	R	L	R	L	R	L

lesson

Kassa

Now that you've learned all the basic strokes, you can start moving through the grooves a lot faster. In this lesson you're going to learn variations on one of the most popular djembe patterns in all of West Africa. It's a part from Kassa, a rhythm from Guinea traditionally played at harvest time to accompany workers in the fields. We'll teach you this groove step by step, building off the basic groove you learned in lesson 1. Here it is again:

PATTERN 1-6

1	+	2	+	3	+	4	+	1	+	2	+	3	+	4	+
✳	•	•	•	△	•	•	•	✳	•	•	•	△	•	•	•
R	L	R	L	R	L	R	L	R	L	R	L	R	L	R	L

As a first step, you're going to add a slap with your left hand on the AND of 2 in each measure. These extra slaps introduce and reinforce the backbeats that follow them. If you're right-handed (as ninety percent of us are) it may feel awkward at first to start each pair of slaps with your left hand. That's because your left hand would rather follow than lead. But you'll get used to it:

PATTERN 2-1

1	+	2	+	3	+	4	+	1	+	2	+	3	+	4	+
✳	•	•	△	△	•	•	•	✳	•	•	△	△	•	•	•
R	L	R	L	R	L	R	L	R	L	R	L	R	L	R	L

Now add two tones at the end of each measure. Pay attention to technique. Try to make your slaps and tones as distinct from each other as possible. And try to make each stroke sound the same in both hands. It may help to close your eyes so you can really listen:

PLAYING
PRINCIPLE

Try to make each stroke sound the same in both hands.

1	+	2	+	3	+	4	+	1	+	2	+	3	+	4	+
✳	•	•	▲	▲	•	O	O	✳	•	•	▲	▲	•	O	O
R	L	R	L	R	L	R	L	R	L	R	L	R	L	R	L

When you replace the basses on 1 with slaps, you're playing the actual part from Kassa. The only difference is that in a traditional West African ensemble this part would be played without the touches. In that context – with other interlocking drum and bell parts filling out the groove – touches would only clutter the sound. But when you have to carry the groove all by yourself, the touches fill in the empty spaces and create a richer, more textured groove:

PATTERN 2-3

1	+	2	+	3	+	4	+	1	+	2	+	3	+	4	+
▲	•	•	▲	▲	•	O	O	▲	•	•	▲	▲	•	O	O
R	L	R	L	R	L	R	L	R	L	R	L	R	L	R	L

Here's the part charted in 4/4:

PATTERN 2-3 (IN 4/4)

1	e	+	a	2	e	+	a	3	e	+	a	4	e	+	a
▲	•	•	▲	▲	•	O	O	▲	•	•	▲	▲	•	O	O
R	L	R	L	R	L	R	L	R	L	R	L	R	L	R	L

The context you're playing in will determine whether it's better to play the pattern with a bass or a slap on 1. If you need more bite, go with the slap. If you need more bottom, go with the bass. For maximum bottom, you can even play a bass on every pulse:

PATTERN 2-4

1	+	2	+	3	+	4	+	1	+	2	+	3	+	4	+
✳	•	•	Δ	✳	•	O	O	✳	•	•	Δ	✳	•	O	O
R	L	R	L	R	L	R	L	R	L	R	L	R	L	R	L

The faster you play this pattern, the smaller your hand and arm movements need to be. One way to maximize your speed and efficiency is to play your bass strokes close to the edge of the drumhead. This means your palm will land in the open tone zone, minimizing the forward and backward motion of the arm.

You can also maximize speed and efficiency on *all* your strokes by minimizing the up-and-down motion of your arms. Keep your hands low – as close to the drumhead as possible. Experienced drummers sometimes do raise their hands high in the air when they play a solo to play louder or to create a dramatic effect. But extra arm motion can compromise speed and accuracy, and – especially with a beginner – can lead to injury. So play close, at least for now.

Now watch what happens when you take out the basses on the backbeats and replace them with touches. This shifts the spotlight to the slaps on the AND of 2 and gives the new pattern an edgier, more suspended feel. That's because these prominent slaps fall on **offbeats** – which in cut-time are all the ANDs:

PLAYING PRINCIPLE

To maximize speed and efficiency, play bass strokes close to the edge of the drumhead.

PLAYING PRINCIPLE

To maximize speed and efficiency, keep your hands close to the drumhead.

PATTERN 2-5

1	+	2	+	3	+	4	+	1	+	2	+	3	+	4	+
✳	•	•	Δ	•	•	O	O	✳	•	•	Δ	•	•	O	O
R	L	R	L	R	L	R	L	R	L	R	L	R	L	R	L

Musical Time-Out: Offbeats and upbeats

The terms **offbeat** and **upbeat** are related. Our definition of an offbeat is any beat that falls off the pulse – *except* for upbeats, which are the beats that fall exactly midway between pulses. This means that in cut-time, the offbeats are all the ANDs and the upbeats fall on 2 and 4:

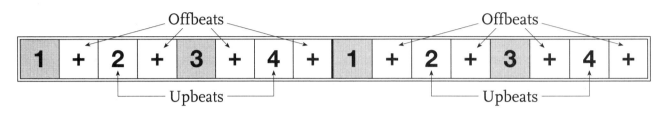

The next pattern is the same as the last except we've added two slaps in the second measure to create a fill:

PATTERN 2-6

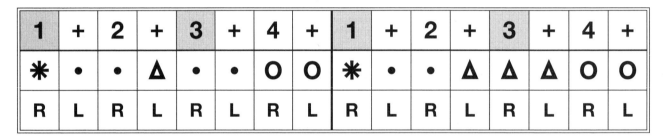

In the next pattern we've put back the slap on the first backbeat:

PATTERN 2-7

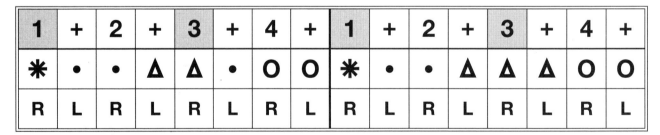

Now we've left everything the same except we've taken out the slap on the second backbeat. That leaves two slaps in the second measure surrounding the backbeat without touching it:

PATTERN 2-8

1	+	2	+	3	+	4	+	1	+	2	+	3	+	4	+
✳	•	•	Δ	Δ	•	O	O	✳	•	•	Δ	•	Δ	O	O
R	L	R	L	R	L	R	L	R	L	R	L	R	L	R	L

lesson  **3**

Straight-eighth feel

In every pattern you've played so far, each pulse has been divided into four beats:

4 Beats

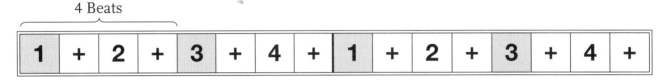

In the patterns in this lesson, each pulse is divided into only *two* beats. We indicate that by shading every numbered beat on the count row:

2 Beats

When the pulse is divided into only two beats, it gives a pattern what's called a **straight-eighth feel**. Millions of rock songs are played this way, with the drummer playing straight eighth notes on the hi-hat or ride cymbal. The patterns in this lesson are designed to allow you to re-create this feel on a hand drum. You can also use a straight-eighth feel whenever a song is moving too fast for you to comfortably play four notes to each pulse.

Musical Time-Out: 4/4 and the straight-eighth feel

If you've been counting in 4/4, you can think of our straight-eighth charts as being compressed versions of our 4/4 charts. All that's different is that we've taken out the "e's" and the "a's." The pulses still fall on every numbered beat:

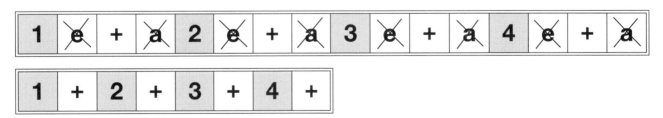

Since there's no difference between a cut-time chart modified for a straight-eighth feel and a 4/4 chart modified for a straight-eighth feel, we won't need to include any extra charts in this lesson.

The first straight-eighth groove is just a compressed version of pattern 1-6. All we did was take out two of the three touches between pulses. To make sure you change from feeling the pulse on 1 and 3 to feeling it on every numbered beat, tap the pulse in your foot while you play:

PATTERN 1-6

1	+	2	+	3	+	4	+	1	+	2	+	3	+	4	+
✳	•	•	△	•	•	✳	•	•	△	•	•
R	L	R	L	R	L	R	L	R	L	R	L	R	L	R	L

PATTERN 3-1

1	+	2	+	3	+	4	+	1	+	2	+	3	+	4	+
✳	•	△	•	✳	•	△	•	✳	•	△	•	✳	•	△	•
R	L	R	L	R	L	R	L	R	L	R	L	R	L	R	L

Notice that the slaps in the compressed pattern are still on the backbeats – every second pulse:

PATTERN 3-1

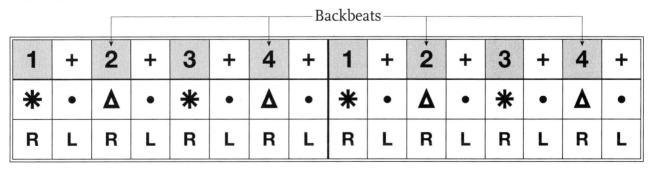

THE PATTERNS - LESSON 3   35

This basic straight-eighth groove is the foundation for the variations that follow. They'll probably sound familiar because they're adaptations of popular drumset patterns. While you play them, you can think of each bass stroke as a stroke on the bass drum, each slap as a rimshot on the snare, and each touch as a tap on the hi-hat.

PRACTICE
PRINCIPLE

Practice with
recorded music.

These grooves – more than any others in this book – are designed exclusively to accompany other instruments rather than to stand on their own. So if you haven't yet tried playing along with recorded music, this would be a great time to start.

When you're a beginner, playing along with recorded music is often the only way to get the feel of what it's like to play in a band. It's also a great way to develop steady time and learn how to listen to other parts while holding your own. And it's a whole lot of fun. Thanks to our CD player, we've had the pleasure of playing with Santana, Sting, Angelique Kidjo, and Youssou N'Dour, and none of them has ever complained about our playing. So pick your favorite music and play along.

For your first variation, start by adding a bass in the left hand on the AND of 2. In this pattern – and in all the variations that follow – it helps to keep your left hand above the drumhead between strokes. That way you'll avoid unnecessary back and forth movements and you'll always be in position for either a bass or a touch:

PATTERN 3-2

1	+	2	+	3	+	4	+	1	+	2	+	3	+	4	+
✳	•	△	✳	✳	•	△	•	✳	•	△	✳	✳	•	△	•
R	L	R	L	R	L	R	L	R	L	R	L	R	L	R	L

Next move the extra bass to the AND of 3. That means the pair of basses now starts in the *right* hand instead of the left:

PATTERN 3-3

1	+	2	+	3	+	4	+	1	+	2	+	3	+	4	+
✳	•	Δ	•	✳	✳	Δ	•	✳	•	Δ	•	✳	✳	Δ	•
R	L	R	L	R	L	R	L	R	L	R	L	R	L	R	L

Now keep the extra bass on the AND of 3 in both measures and add another bass on the AND of 4 in the second measure. Notice that you start the first pair of basses in the second measure with your right hand and the second pair with your left:

PATTERN 3-4

1	+	2	+	3	+	4	+	1	+	2	+	3	+	4	+
✳	•	Δ	•	✳	✳	Δ	•	✳	•	Δ	•	✳	✳	Δ	✳
R	L	R	L	R	L	R	L	R	L	R	L	R	L	R	L

Musical Time-Out: Upbeats in a straight-eighth feel

Remember in the last lesson we said that upbeats are the beats that fall exactly midway between pulses? In cut-time, that meant beats 2 and 4. When you go from cut-time to a straight-eighth feel, the upbeats become the ANDs because they fall exactly midway between the pulses on every numbered beat:

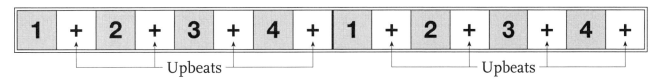

Notice that since the single box between each two pulses is an upbeat, on our straight-eighth charts there aren't any offbeats.

In the next variation, your left hand plays basses on three upbeats in a row, starting on the AND of 2 in each measure. If you find it more comfortable to leave out the touch on 3, go ahead. Just make sure you've got the timing right by listening to the CD:

PATTERN 3-5

1	+	2	+	3	+	4	+	1	+	2	+	3	+	4	+
✳	•	△	✳	•	✳	△	✳	✳	•	△	✳	•	✳	△	✳
R	L	R	L	R	L	R	L	R	L	R	L	R	L	R	L

If you want to create a more open sound, you can thin out this pattern by leaving out the bass on the AND of 4:

PATTERN 3-6

1	+	2	+	3	+	4	+	1	+	2	+	3	+	4	+
✳	•	△	✳	•	✳	△	•	✳	•	△	✳	•	✳	△	•
R	L	R	L	R	L	R	L	R	L	R	L	R	L	R	L

Another way to thin out pattern 3-5 is to leave out the bass on the AND of 2:

PATTERN 3-7

1	+	2	+	3	+	4	+	1	+	2	+	3	+	4	+
✳	•	△	•	•	✳	△	✳	✳	•	△	•	•	✳	△	✳
R	L	R	L	R	L	R	L	R	L	R	L	R	L	R	L

The next variation is even thinner, with a bass in the left hand only on the AND of 3:

PATTERN 3-8

1	+	2	+	3	+	4	+	1	+	2	+	3	+	4	+
✳	•	Δ	•	•	✳	Δ	•	✳	•	Δ	•	•	✳	Δ	•
R	L	R	L	R	L	R	L	R	L	R	L	R	L	R	L

To keep things interesting, you'll probably want to combine these variations. In the next chart, the first measure is pattern 3-7 and the second is pattern 3-8:

PATTERN 3-9   `PLAY-ALONG`

1	+	2	+	3	+	4	+	1	+	2	+	3	+	4	+
✳	•	Δ	•	•	✳	Δ	✳	✳	•	Δ	•	•	✳	Δ	•
R	L	R	L	R	L	R	L	R	L	R	L	R	L	R	L

Now put on your favorite rock CD and try combining these variations in your own way. If you discover some combinations that you don't want to forget, you can write them down on the blank charts at the back of the book.

lesson

One-bar clave

All dance music is organized around a steady pulse. But African and Afro-Cuban rhythms are also organized around *asymmetrical* repeating rhythmic patterns called **timelines**. The musicians in a group use the timeline as their reference rhythm and play their parts in relation to it.

In Afro-Cuban rhythms, the timeline is called the **clave** (klah-vay) and it's usually played on two cylindrical pieces of wood called claves:

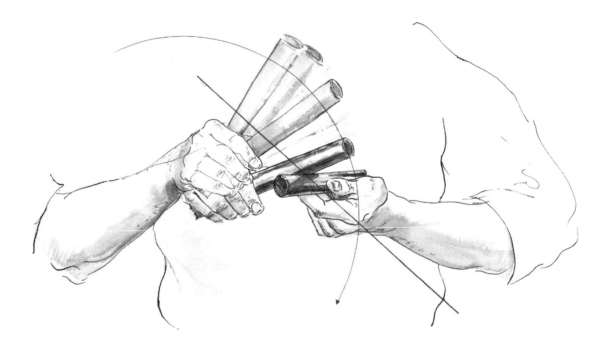

Claves are ideal for timelines because they produce crisp, penetrating sounds that can be heard above other instruments.

The grooves in this lesson are based on a timeline called the one-bar clave. This popular rhythmic pattern can be found in music all over the world. In cut-time, the one-bar clave is only one measure long. That means it will repeat twice on our two-measure charts.

In the first pattern, you'll play the one-bar clave with basses, filling in the beats in between with touches. Notice that since we're back in cut-time, the pulse is back on 1 and 3:

PATTERN 4-1

One-bar clave

1	+	2	+	3	+	4	+	1	+	2	+	3	+	4	+
✳	•	•	✳	•	•	✳	•	✳	•	•	✳	•	•	✳	•
R	L	R	L	R	L	R	L	R	L	R	L	R	L	R	L

Here's how the same pattern looks in 4/4:

PATTERN 4-1 (IN 4/4)

1	e	+	a	2	e	+	a	3	e	+	a	4	e	+	a
✳	•	•	✳	•	•	✳	•	✳	•	•	✳	•	•	✳	•
R	L	R	L	R	L	R	L	R	L	R	L	R	L	R	L

The one-bar clave gets its tremendous vitality from its uneven-ness.
It's like a wheel that's not quite round; it's got a hitch in it. Exactly
three beats after the first note comes the second note, and exactly three
beats after the second note comes the third. Then comes the hitch.
After only *two* beats, the pattern abruptly starts over again on 1:

PATTERN 4-1

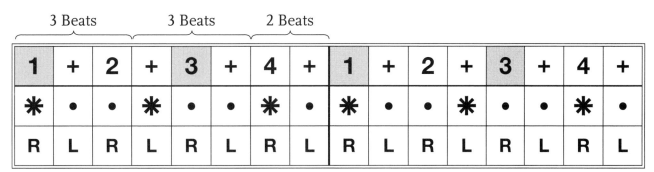

	3 Beats				3 Beats				2 Beats						
1	+	2	+	3	+	4	+	1	+	2	+	3	+	4	+
✳	•	•	✳	•	•	✳	•	✳	•	•	✳	•	•	✳	•
R	L	R	L	R	L	R	L	R	L	R	L	R	L	R	L

Now vary the pattern by replacing the bass on the AND of 2 with a slap.

PATTERN 4-2

1	+	2	+	3	+	4	+	1	+	2	+	3	+	4	+
✱	•	•	Δ	•	•	✱	•	✱	•	•	Δ	•	•	✱	•
R	L	R	L	R	L	R	L	R	L	R	L	R	L	R	L

Now substitute one of the Kassa variations for the second measure:

PATTERN 4-3

1	+	2	+	3	+	4	+	1	+	2	+	3	+	4	+
✱	•	•	Δ	•	•	✱	•	✱	•	•	Δ	Δ	•	O	O
R	L	R	L	R	L	R	L	R	L	R	L	R	L	R	L

The next pattern is the same as the last except we've filled in the AND of 3 in the second measure with another slap:

PATTERN 4-4

1	+	2	+	3	+	4	+	1	+	2	+	3	+	4	+
✱	•	•	Δ	•	•	✱	•	✱	•	•	Δ	Δ	Δ	O	O
R	L	R	L	R	L	R	L	R	L	R	L	R	L	R	L

Now combine the last two patterns to create a longer phrase:

PATTERN 4-5

1	+	2	+	3	+	4	+	1	+	2	+	3	+	4	+
✳	•	•	Δ	•	•	✳	•	✳	•	•	Δ	Δ	•	O	O
R	L	R	L	R	L	R	L	R	L	R	L	R	L	R	L

1	+	2	+	3	+	4	+	1	+	2	+	3	+	4	+
✳	•	•	Δ	•	•	✳	•	✳	•	•	Δ	Δ	Δ	O	O
R	L	R	L	R	L	R	L	R	L	R	L	R	L	R	L

The next pattern is designed to prepare you for the patterns that follow it. The idea is to get you comfortable with the hand pattern before you combine it with a measure of the one-bar clave. This is the first time you've played the sequence slap-tone-tone-slap, so take your time at first:

PATTERN 4-6

1	+	2	+	3	+	4	+	1	+	2	+	3	+	4	+
✳	Δ	O	O	Δ	•	O	O	✳	Δ	O	O	Δ	•	O	O
R	L	R	L	R	L	R	L	R	L	R	L	R	L	R	L

The first measure of the next pattern is the one-bar clave played with bass strokes. The second measure is the pattern you just played. You can think of the pattern as consisting of two phrases or as a call and response – the basses are the call and the slaps and tones are the response:

1	+	2	+	3	+	4	+	1	+	2	+	3	+	4	+
✳	•	•	✳	•	•	✳	•	✳	Δ	O	O	Δ	•	O	O
R	L	R	L	R	L	R	L	R	L	R	L	R	L	R	L

The next pattern is the same as the last except we've taken out the bass on 1 in the second measure. This creates more space between the call and the response:

PATTERN 4-8

1	+	2	+	3	+	4	+	1	+	2	+	3	+	4	+
✳	•	•	✳	•	•	✳	•	•	Δ	O	O	Δ	•	O	O
R	L	R	L	R	L	R	L	R	L	R	L	R	L	R	L

Now fill in the empty beat in the response by adding a slap on the AND of 3 in the second measure:

PATTERN 4-9

1	+	2	+	3	+	4	+	1	+	2	+	3	+	4	+
✳	•	•	✳	•	•	✳	•	•	Δ	O	O	Δ	Δ	O	O
R	L	R	L	R	L	R	L	R	L	R	L	R	L	R	L

Now combine the last two patterns to create a longer phrase:

PATTERN 4-10

PLAY-ALONG

1	+	2	+	3	+	4	+	1	+	2	+	3	+	4	+
✳	•	•	✳	•	•	✳	•	•	Δ	O	O	Δ	•	O	O
R	L	R	L	R	L	R	L	R	L	R	L	R	L	R	L

1	+	2	+	3	+	4	+	1	+	2	+	3	+	4	+
✳	•	•	✳	•	•	✳	•	•	Δ	O	O	Δ	Δ	O	O
R	L	R	L	R	L	R	L	R	L	R	L	R	L	R	L

We hope by now you've settled into some kind of regular practice routine. Here are some tips for making sure your practice sessions are pleasurable as well as productive.

The first thing to think about is your practice space. Find a place that's comfortable and inviting where you can make a lot of noise. Then clean it up. Get rid of the clutter. Make it beautiful, so you'll want to spend time there.

If possible, set aside a regular time to practice. Make it a ritual. If you have the flexibility in your schedule, pick the time of day when your energy is good and your hands feel the best.

Make practicing a ritual.

When it's practice time, change into comfortable clothes. Do what you can to protect yourself from distractions, like the phone, roommates, kids. Then take a minute to settle in. Stretch. Breathe. Focus.

Begin each practice session with a warm-up. Play gently at first, starting with bass strokes and tones before adding slaps. Feel your way into the drum.

PRACTICE
PRINCIPLE

Isolate difficult
parts of a pattern
and practice them
separately.

Once you've limbered up, then start working on your lesson. If you find yourself stumbling when you try to play a pattern fast, go back to playing it slow. If one part of a pattern is tripping you up, isolate it and practice it separately. If you're still having trouble, put your hands in your lap, close your eyes, and visualize yourself playing the pattern correctly. If that doesn't work, try practicing something else or take a break. Come back to the pattern when you're fresh.

PRACTICE
PRINCIPLE

Don't grind in
mistakes.

Whatever you do, don't grind in mistakes. Playing a pattern incorrectly over and over only teaches your body to play it incorrectly. And don't beat yourself up either. Everybody makes mistakes. The key is learning how not to repeat them.

Once you can play a pattern correctly, shift your focus to technique. Really listen to yourself play. The tones should be clear and the slaps crisp, even when you play fast. And your strokes should sound the same in both hands. If there's a difference, analyze what your strong hand is doing and mimic it in the other hand. Let your strong hand teach your weak hand how to play.

PRACTICE
PRINCIPLE

Let your strong hand
teach your weak
hand how to play.

It's a good idea to include some review every time you practice. Reviewing reminds you that you're competent and you'll discover something new in these rhythms every time you play them.

Whenever you have a long practice session, take breaks to stretch and refresh yourself. Quit while you still have energy and end on a high note.

lesson

Hip-hop

Whenever you want to adapt a drumset pattern to a hand drum, there are two ways to handle the bass drum part. The first way – and the most obvious – is to replace notes that would have been played on the bass drum of a drumset with bass strokes on a hand drum. That's what we've been doing so far. The second way is to use open tones instead.

In this lesson, we're going to use a combination of bass strokes and open tones to replace the bass drum part of some hip-hop drumset patterns. We're going to keep a bass stroke on ONE – the first beat in the first measure – to firmly anchor the grooves. But in the middle of the patterns we'll use open tones instead. Those open tones will fall in the zone from the AND of 4 in the first measure to beat 2 in the second. To get to know that zone, start by playing tones on every one of those beats. Notice you play the first tone with your left hand:

PATTERN 5-1

1	+	2	+	3	+	4	+	1	+	2	+	3	+	4	+
✳	•	•	•	△	•	•	O	O	O	O	•	△	•	•	•
R	L	R	L	R	L	R	L	R	L	R	L	R	L	R	L

When you take out the tone on 1 in the second measure, things start to get funkier. The funkiness comes from the contrast between the bass *on* the pulse at the start of the first measure and the tones dancing *around* the pulse at the start of the second. On a drumset, all these notes would be played on the bass drum:

PATTERN 5-2

1	+	2	+	3	+	4	+	1	+	2	+	3	+	4	+
✳	•	•	•	△	•	•	O	•	O	O	•	△	•	•	•
R	L	R	L	R	L	R	L	R	L	R	L	R	L	R	L

1	e	+	a	2	e	+	a	3	e	+	a	4	e	+	a
✳	•	•	•	Δ	•	•	O	•	O	O	•	Δ	•	•	•
R	L	R	L	R	L	R	L	R	L	R	L	R	L	R	L

Now add two open tones at the end of the pattern as a fill:

PATTERN 5-3

1	+	2	+	3	+	4	+	1	+	2	+	3	+	4	+
✳	•	•	•	Δ	•	•	O	•	O	O	•	Δ	•	O	O
R	L	R	L	R	L	R	L	R	L	R	L	R	L	R	L

This is a great groove to play with a **funk swing feel**. In four, this feel is created by playing the notes on the ANDS slightly closer to the numbered beats. The best way to understand this concept is by listening to the CD. We've also indicated the swing on the next chart:

PATTERN 5-4

1	+	2	+	3	+	4	+	1	+	2	+	3	+	4	+
✳	•	•	•	Δ	•	•	O	•	O	O	•	Δ	•	O	O
R	L	R	L	R	L	R	L	R	L	R	L	R	L	R	L

You can try adding a swing to just about any pattern. How far the notes on the ANDS are swung varies from rhythm to rhythm and drummer to drummer. Go ahead and experiment to find the amount that feels good to you. Just make sure you don't swing out of control and fall off your chair.

**Find the amount of swing feels good to you.
Just make sure you don't swing out of control
and fall off your chair.**

In the next pattern, we've added another bass on 2 in the first measure. Although we haven't indicated the swing feel on the chart, you should play this pattern and all the rest of the patterns in this lesson with a swing. You'll also hear the patterns played that way on the CD:

PATTERN 5-5

1	+	2	+	3	+	4	+	1	+	2	+	3	+	4	+
✳	•	✳	•	Δ	•	•	O	•	O	O	•	Δ	•	O	O
R	L	R	L	R	L	R	L	R	L	R	L	R	L	R	L

The next pattern illustrates how you can dramatically change the character of the "bass drum" part by changing one note. When you replace the bass on 2 in the first measure with a tone, the pattern becomes more melodic. As you go from bass to tone to slap in the first measure, the rising pitches make the drum sound almost like a bass guitar:

PATTERN 5-6

1	+	2	+	3	+	4	+	1	+	2	+	3	+	4	+
✳	•	O	•	Δ	•	•	O	•	O	O	•	Δ	•	O	O
R	L	R	L	R	L	R	L	R	L	R	L	R	L	R	L

Your decision to use a bass or a tone as a "bass drum" stroke will depend on a number of factors, including how loud your drum is, what other instruments are being played, and what kind of sound you're looking for. Bass strokes give you more bottom, but their sound can get buried by other instruments. Tones cut through better, but they can overcrowd the available sonic space. Tones can also clash with other pitched instruments because they have the most distinct pitch of any sound on a hand drum. Ideally, you should know the "bass drum" part in a groove well enough to be able to go either way, depending on the situation.

Now create a longer phrase by combining patterns 5-4 and 5-6. You'll hear a short version of this pattern played with the rest of the patterns in this lesson on the CD. And since it's the play-along pattern for this lesson, you'll also find a two-minute version of it at the end of track 5:

PATTERN 5-7

PLAY-ALONG

1	+	2	+	3	+	4	+	1	+	2	+	3	+	4	+
✳	•	•	•	Δ	•	•	O	•	O	O	•	Δ	•	O	O
R	L	R	L	R	L	R	L	R	L	R	L	R	L	R	L

1	+	2	+	3	+	4	+	1	+	2	+	3	+	4	+
✳	•	O	•	Δ	•	•	O	•	O	O	•	Δ	•	O	O
R	L	R	L	R	L	R	L	R	L	R	L	R	L	R	L

The next pattern is similar to the patterns you've been playing except that we've shifted the "tone zone" one beat to the left. Instead of starting on the AND of 4 in the first measure, it now starts on 4 and extends through the AND of 1 in the second measure:

PATTERN 5-8

1	+	2	+	3	+	4	+	1	+	2	+	3	+	4	+
✳	•	•	•	Δ	•	O	O	O	O	•	•	Δ	•	O	O
R	L	R	L	R	L	R	L	R	L	R	L	R	L	R	L

Now we want to add another groove tool to your toolbox. It's a technique called the drop and it's always played on the beat before a slap. To play a drop simply place one hand on the drumhead and keep it there while you play a slap with the other hand. The weight of the dropped hand momentarily tightens the drumhead and suppresses the overtones, making the slap that follows drier and crisper.

When you play a drop, your hand should make contact with the drumhead at the base of the palm and the pads of the fingertips simultaneously. This will happen naturally if your hand is relaxed.

Try a drop now in the pattern you just played. When you get to the AND of 2 in each measure, simply place your left hand on the drumhead. Then leave it there while you play the slap on the backbeat that follows. Then just lift the fingertips of your left hand and drop them again to play the touch on the AND of 3:

$\overset{\bullet}{\smile}$ = drop

The symbol for the drop is a combination of the symbols for the heel and the toe, which both make contact with the drumhead simultaneously.

PATTERN 5-9

1	+	2	+	3	+	4	+	1	+	2	+	3	+	4	+
✳	•	•	$\overset{\bullet}{\smile}$	△	•	O	O	O	O	•	$\overset{\bullet}{\smile}$	△	•	O	O
R	L	R	L	R	L	R	L	R	L	R	L	R	L	R	L

Fun, huh? If you like what the drop does to the sound of your slap, you can try using it in other patterns. You can use it before an open slap – where your fingers bounce off the head immediately – or a closed slap – where your fingers grip and remain on the drumhead. The only time you can't use it is when you need to play a main stroke with the dropped hand right after the slap. Then there just isn't time.

lesson **6**

Kpanlogo

The patterns in this lesson are based on support drum parts from a traditional rhythm from Ghana called Kpanlogo (pahn-loh-goh). To make them work as stand-alone grooves, we've added timekeeping strokes using a technique called the heel-toe.

The heel-toe is typically used by conga drummers, but it works well on any drum. It involves a rocking motion between the chubby part of the palm – the "heel" – and the fingers – the "toe." Some people call this technique the "heel-tip" or "palm-finger." We're all describing the same thing.

To make a heel stroke, hold your hand an inch or so above the drumhead and simply drop your wrist so that the heel makes contact with the drumhead while you keep the rest of your hand and fingers up. Don't let your wrist make contact with the drum:

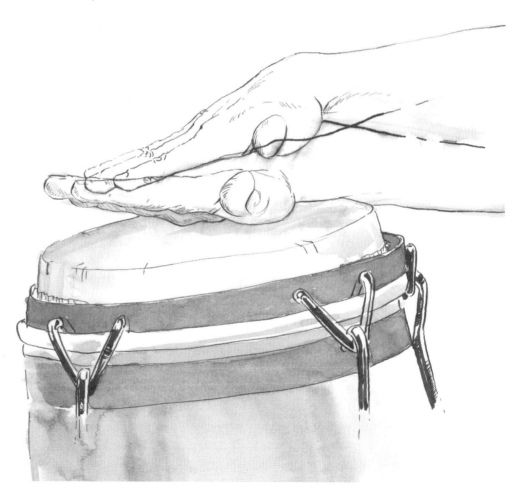

◖ = heel stroke

Now, with the heel of your palm still on the drumhead, just drop your fingers and you've completed a heel-toe. The toe stroke is just a touch that goes with a heel stroke.

You can play a heel-toe anywhere on the drumhead. The exact location will depend on what strokes come before and after it. For the patterns in this lesson, you'll be playing it with your palms close to the edge of the drumhead.

You can play heel-toes heavy or light, loud or soft, depending on the effect you want. For now, we'll be using them primarily as time-keepers, so they should be played lightly.

When you play a series of heel-toes, your hand will rock back and forth like a seesaw. When the heel goes down, the fingers come up; when the fingers go down, the heel comes up. Now try this rocking motion with your right hand, keeping your wrist and hand loose and relaxed:

MEMORY TIP

Since the toe and the touch are the same stroke, the symbol for both is the same.

• = toe

PATTERN 6-1

1	+	2	+	3	+	4	+	1	+	2	+	3	+	4	+
ᴗ	•	ᴗ	•	ᴗ	•	ᴗ	•	ᴗ	•	ᴗ	•	ᴗ	•	ᴗ	•
R	R	R	R	R	R	R	R	R	R	R	R	R	R	R	R

Now try it with your left:

PATTERN 6-1

1	+	2	+	3	+	4	+	1	+	2	+	3	+	4	+
ᴗ	•	ᴗ	•	ᴗ	•	ᴗ	•	ᴗ	•	ᴗ	•	ᴗ	•	ᴗ	•
L	L	L	L	L	L	L	L	L	L	L	L	L	L	L	L

Now that you know how to play heel-toes with each hand separately, you're ready to put your hands together to play what we call the basic heel-toe. It goes heel-heel-toe-toe with alternating hands.

1	+	2	+	3	+	4	+	1	+	2	+	3	+	4	+
⌣	⌣	•	•	⌣	⌣	•	•	⌣	⌣	•	•	⌣	⌣	•	•
R	L	R	L	R	L	R	L	R	L	R	L	R	L	R	L

When you really get going on this one, the rocking motion becomes less pronounced. Neither the heel nor toe remains in contact with the drumhead for more than an instant. At high speed, the pattern starts to sound like a train going by in the distance. At super high speed, it can sound like the purring of a cat.

As timekeeping strokes, heel-toes have several advantages over touches. First, they're a lot less tiring over long stretches because you get two strokes for the price of one: the heel hits as the wrist goes down and the fingers hit automatically as the wrist comes up. Second, they're more relaxing because you get to rest momentarily each time you play a heel stroke; pure touches leave you hanging. Third, heel-toes create a more varied texture than pure touches because the heels add bottom to the pattern. And fourth, heel-toes make it easier for you to keep your place in a pattern because the more varied sequence of strokes gives you more reference points.

Now we want to add another groove tool to your toolbox: the *shifted* heel-toe. We'll teach it to you in two steps. Start by playing the basic heel-toe pattern, but this time start with your left hand instead of your right:

PATTERN 6-2

1	+	2	+	3	+	4	+	1	+	2	+	3	+	4	+
⌣	⌣	•	•	⌣	⌣	•	•	⌣	⌣	•	•	⌣	⌣	•	•
L	R	L	R	L	R	L	R	L	R	L	R	L	R	L	R

To get the shifted heel-toe, all you have to do is shift this pattern one beat to the left. This puts the right heel on each pulse and bumps the left heel onto the beat *before* each pulse. The left heel that was on ONE is now on the AND of 4 in the second measure, and each pair of heels ends on a pulse: "AND 1, and 2, AND 3, and 4, AND 1 ..."

To feel the difference shifting makes in this pattern, you need to have the pulse going in your body. So before you start playing, make sure you're already tapping your foot or doing whatever you do to feel the pulse:

PATTERN 6-3

1	+	2	+	3	+	4	+	1	+	2	+	3	+	4	+
⌣	•	•	⌣	⌣	•	•	⌣	⌣	•	•	⌣	⌣	•	•	⌣
R	L	R	L	R	L	R	L	R	L	R	L	R	L	R	L

PATTERN 6-3 (IN 4/4)

1	e	+	a	2	e	+	a	3	e	+	a	4	e	+	a
⌣	•	•	⌣	⌣	•	•	⌣	⌣	•	•	⌣	⌣	•	•	⌣
R	L	R	L	R	L	R	L	R	L	R	L	R	L	R	L

Could you feel the effect of the shift? In its new position, the left heel is able to give the pulse a push. This rhythm – when played loudly on a bass drum – is the heart of the samba.

It only takes a subtle adjustment in the flow of your hands to add a slap on the backbeat to the shifted heel-toe. To get a crisp slap, leave your left hand on the drumhead after you play the heel on the AND of 2. You may find it helpful to start playing the pattern without the slap at first just to get your hands flowing:

PATTERN 6-4

1	+	2	+	3	+	4	+	1	+	2	+	3	+	4	+
⌣	•	•	⌣	△	•	•	⌣	⌣	•	•	⌣	△	•	•	⌣
R	L	R	L	R	L	R	L	R	L	R	L	R	L	R	L

Now for the first part from Kpanlogo. It's just the shifted heel-toe pattern with two tones at the end of each measure:

PATTERN 6-5

1	+	2	+	3	+	4	+	1	+	2	+	3	+	4	+
⌐	•	•	⌐	⌐	•	O	O	⌐	•	•	⌐	⌐	•	O	O
R	L	R	L	R	L	R	L	R	L	R	L	R	L	R	L

We said earlier in this lesson that heel-toes can be played heavy or light. So far you've been playing them lightly, as timekeeping strokes. If you want a heavier sound, you can turn the heels into basses:

PATTERN 6-6

1	+	2	+	3	+	4	+	1	+	2	+	3	+	4	+
✳	•	•	✳	✳	•	O	O	✳	•	•	✳	✳	•	O	O
R	L	R	L	R	L	R	L	R	L	R	L	R	L	R	L

Now you're ready for the second part from Kpanlogo. Remember to play the heel-toes lightly because you're only using them as time-keeping strokes:

PATTERN 6-7   PLAY-ALONG

1	+	2	+	3	+	4	+	1	+	2	+	3	+	4	+
⌐	•	•	⌐	⌐	•	Δ	Δ	O	•	O	O	•	•	Δ	Δ
R	L	R	L	R	L	R	L	R	L	R	L	R	L	R	L

PATTERN 6-7 (IN 4/4)

1	e	+	a	2	e	+	a	3	e	+	a	4	e	+	a
⌐	•	•	⌐	⌐	•	Δ	Δ	O	•	O	O	•	•	Δ	Δ
R	L	R	L	R	L	R	L	R	L	R	L	R	L	R	L

Until this lesson, all the patterns you've played have had familiar sign-posts to keep you oriented in time: a bass on ONE or a slap on the back-beat or both. This Kpanlogo pattern has neither. So you'll need a strong *internal* sense of time to keep your bearings.

And if you're going to play this pattern with other musicians, make sure someone else is responsible for holding down the pulse. No matter how solid you are, don't risk confusing the musicians you're playing with or losing the dancers.

Tumbao rock

Tumbao is the most popular conga pattern in contemporary Latin music. But it's also a versatile groove that fits well with rock, funk, and jazz. Once you learn it, you'll find plenty of opportunities to play it.

The tumbao pattern is pure heel-toe in the left hand, with slaps and tones in the right. Here's the formation your hands should be in when you play it:

Whenever you play a pattern where one hand stays up on the drumhead and the other stays at the edge of the drum, the hands should form a "T."

PLAYING PRINCIPLE

Whenever one hand plays up on the drumhead and the other at the edge of the drum, the hands should form a "T."

To get you ready for tumbao we're going to take you through a couple of exercises. In the first one, all the right hand does is play a slap on each upbeat (2 and 4 in each measure). No problem there. It's the left hand that's tricky, so we want to focus your attention there for a minute before you start playing.

Until now, whenever you've played heel-toes they've served primarily as timekeeping strokes. Not here. In tumbao, the heel-toes in the left hand are an important part of the groove. They shouldn't be played as loud as the strokes in your right hand, but they should be clearly audible.

Another thing to notice is that the left hand gets to play a new sequence of strokes. After each slap, it goes toe-heel-toe. When you get to the heel stroke in that sequence, leave your heel on the drumhead and simply drop your fingers to play the toe stroke that follows. Then leave your hand resting on the drumhead – like a dropped hand – while you play the slap. This will make the slap in the right hand crisper:

PATTERN 7-1

1	+	2	+	3	+	4	+	1	+	2	+	3	+	4	+
◡	•	△	•	◡	•	△	•	◡	•	△	•	◡	•	△	•
L	L	R	L	L	L	R	L	L	L	R	L	L	L	R	L

In the second exercise, the right hand plays two tones in a row – your first double-stroke. The left hand just plays heel-toe. This time, make sure you *lift* your left hand after each heel-toe so you don't muffle the tones that follow:

PATTERN 7-2

1	+	2	+	3	+	4	+	1	+	2	+	3	+	4	+
⌣	•	O	O	⌣	•	O	O	⌣	•	O	O	⌣	•	O	O
L	L	R	R	L	L	R	R	L	L	R	R	L	L	R	R

Now you're ready for the full tumbao. Notice that the sequence in the left hand before the slap goes heel-toe and the sequence before the tones goes *toe*-heel-toe. Each sequence requires a different strategy. To set up a crisp slap, leave your left hand down after you play the heel on 1, drop your fingers to play the toe stroke that follows, and – with your left hand still on the drumhead – play the slap. To get an even crisper sound, play a closed slap, gripping the drumhead momentarily with the fingers of your right hand. Then lift your left hand to play the toe-heel-toe, making sure it's completely off the drumhead when you play the tone on 4:

PATTERN 7-3   ┌─────────────┐
                                                   │ PLAY-ALONG │
                                                   └─────────────┘

1	+	2	+	3	+	4	+	1	+	2	+	3	+	4	+
⌣	•	△	•	⌣	•	O	O	⌣	•	△	•	⌣	•	O	O
L	L	R	L	L	L	R	R	L	L	R	L	L	L	R	R

You'll hear a short version of tumbao played slowly with the rest of the patterns in this lesson on the CD. And since it's the play-along pattern for this lesson, you'll also find a two-minute version of it at the end of track 7. Here it is charted in 4/4:

PATTERN 7-3 (IN 4/4)

1	e	+	a	2	e	+	a	3	e	+	a	4	e	+	a
⌣	•	△	•	⌣	•	O	O	⌣	•	△	•	⌣	•	O	O
L	L	R	L	L	L	R	R	L	L	R	L	L	L	R	R

Tumbao is a great pattern to play along with recorded music because it fits with almost everything. In Latin music, tumbao is played in cut-time – which is how you just played it – with four notes to a pulse. But in up-tempo rock songs, it's played with a straight-eighth feel – with two notes to a pulse. That puts the slap and the first of the two tones on the backbeats. To get the feel of tumbao in a straight-eighth feel, play it the same way you just did only now tap your foot on every numbered beat while you play:

PATTERN 7-3

1	+	2	+	3	+	4	+	1	+	2	+	3	+	4	+
⌣	•	△	•	⌣	•	O	O	⌣	•	△	•	⌣	•	O	O
L	L	R	L	L	L	R	R	L	L	R	L	L	L	R	R

A common straight-eighth drumset variation replaces the two tones with slaps:

PATTERN 7-4

1	+	2	+	3	+	4	+	1	+	2	+	3	+	4	+
⌣	•	△	•	⌣	•	△	△	⌣	•	△	•	⌣	•	△	△
L	L	R	L	L	L	R	R	L	L	R	L	L	L	R	R

Another common straight-eighth drumset variation reverses the order so the two slaps come first followed by the single slap. You'll probably recognize this rhythm from classic rock and roll:

PATTERN 7-5

1	+	2	+	3	+	4	+	1	+	2	+	3	+	4	+
⌣	•	△	△	⌣	•	△	•	⌣	•	△	△	⌣	•	△	•
L	L	R	R	L	L	R	L	L	L	R	R	L	L	R	L

You can add a little extra texture to the straight-eighth tumbao by playing an extra touch in the right hand after the touch in the left hand on the AND of 2. Those two touches are sixteenth notes, which are played twice as fast as eighth notes. We indicate sixteenth notes on our cut-time charts by putting two symbols in one box. Play the first touch on the AND of 2 and the second midway between the AND of 2 and 3. Take your time until you get the feel of the flutter:

PATTERN 7-6

1	+	2	+	3	+	4	+	1	+	2	+	3	+	4	+
⌣	•	△	• •	⌣	•	O	O	⌣	•	△	• •	⌣	•	O	O
L	L	R	LR	L	L	R	R	L	L	R	LR	L	L	R	R

If you don't need the underlying heel-toe groove in the left hand – or if the tempo is too fast for your left hand to play comfortably – you can play the tumbao pattern with alternating hands. That's what you'll do in the next pattern, which is charted in cut-time again. In West African rhythms, this pattern is played without touches as a support drum part. We've added touches to fill out the groove and help you keep steady time. Remember that the first of the two tones is in the right hand:

PATTERN 7-7

1	+	2	+	3	+	4	+	1	+	2	+	3	+	4	+
•	•	△	•	•	•	O	O	•	•	△	•	•	•	O	O
R	L	R	L	R	L	R	L	R	L	R	L	R	L	R	L

The next pattern is a similar West African support drum part. The only difference is that now there's a second slap on the AND of 2 in each measure. This small change in structure makes the pattern a lot more challenging to play – especially at fast tempos. That's because not only are all the main strokes off the pulse, but each pair of slaps and tones ends on an offbeat.

If you're not careful, the magnetic force of the pulse can sneak up on you and pull you off course. After playing for a while at a fast tempo you may start thinking: "Hey, this isn't so hard!" This either means you're a quick learner or you've stopped fighting and without realizing it have surrendered to the pull of the pulse.

The touches should help keep you on track, but we still recommend that you tap your foot while you play this pattern. Then you can make sure that the touch in your right hand hits the drum at the same time as your foot hits the floor. It may also help to think of each pair of slaps or tones as leading into the pulse that follows in your foot.

You'll notice that the slaps in the pattern on the CD are played as open slaps:

PATTERN 7-8

1	+	2	+	3	+	4	+	1	+	2	+	3	+	4	+
•	•	Δ	Δ	•	•	O	O	•	•	Δ	Δ	•	•	O	O
R	L	R	L	R	L	R	L	R	L	R	L	R	L	R	L

Before you play this pattern with a group, make sure that someone else is holding down the pulse. Otherwise you may pull everyone off course. If you like the pattern but need to make it less ambiguous, you can add a bass on 1:

PATTERN 7-9

1	+	2	+	3	+	4	+	1	+	2	+	3	+	4	+
✳	•	Δ	Δ	•	•	O	O	✳	•	Δ	Δ	•	•	O	O
R	L	R	L	R	L	R	L	R	L	R	L	R	L	R	L

lesson **8**

Paradiddle funk

In this lesson, we're going to take a popular sticking sequence used by drumset players – called a **paradiddle** – and apply it to the hand drum to create some funky grooves. You're going to start the paradiddle with your left hand and play eight strokes in the following order: LRLL-RLRR.

Since the sequence has eight strokes, it will repeat twice on our two-measure charts. Your hands will be in the same "T" formation they were in for tumbao. And just as in tumbao, the left hand will play heavy heel-toes while the right hand takes the lead.

Before you tackle the full paradiddle, start by repeating just the first five strokes. Leave your left hand on the drumhead after the touch on the AND of 2 so you'll get a nice, crisp slap on the backbeat:

PATTERN 8-1

1	+	2	+	3	+	4	+	1	+	2	+	3	+	4	+
ᵕ	•	ᵕ	•	▲				ᵕ	•	ᵕ	•	▲			
L	R	L	L	R				L	R	L	L	R			

Now add a touch and two tones in the second half of each measure to complete the pattern. To make it come to life, add a little swing too. You'll hear that swing in all the paradiddle funk patterns on the CD:

PATTERN 8-2

1	+	2	+	3	+	4	+	1	+	2	+	3	+	4	+
ᵕ	•	ᵕ	•	▲	•	O	O	ᵕ	•	ᵕ	•	▲	•	O	O
L	R	L	L	R	L	R	R	L	R	L	L	R	L	R	R

1	e	+	a	2	e	+	a	3	e	+	a	4	e	+	a
⌣	•	⌣	•	△	•	O	O	⌣	•	⌣	•	△	•	O	O
L	R	L	L	R	L	R	R	L	R	L	L	R	L	R	R

The next pattern is the same as the last except that we've added another tone in the right hand on the AND of 1 in the second measure:

PATTERN 8-3

1	+	2	+	3	+	4	+	1	+	2	+	3	+	4	+
⌣	•	⌣	•	△	•	O	O	⌣	O	⌣	•	△	•	O	O
L	R	L	L	R	L	R	R	L	R	L	L	R	L	R	R

Although paradiddle grooves sound funky and feel great to play, they have one drawback: they offer limited possibilities for variation. This is true of any groove played in the "T" formation where both hands are locked into limited roles. That's why for most songs, you'll probably want to combine paradiddle funk patterns with patterns that use alternating hands.

Here's how it's done. To go from a paradiddle pattern to a pattern that uses alternating hands, all you need to do is play the last note of the paradiddle pattern with your *left* hand instead of your right. Then you're all set to start an alternating-hands pattern with your *right*.

To make it easier for you to see how this transition works, we've connected three charts on the next page. The first chart is the paradiddle pattern you just got done playing. On the CD, you'll hear it played just once, but you may want to start by playing it over and over until you're in the groove.

When you're ready to switch, move on to the second chart, which is the same as the paradiddle pattern except that it ends with the *left* hand. Don't repeat that chart. Just play it straight through once and continue on to the third chart.

The third chart is one of the Kassa grooves you played in lesson 2 – a pattern that uses alternating hands. On the CD, you'll hear it repeated twice, but you can repeat it for as long as you like. In just a minute, we'll show you how to switch back to the paradiddle pattern.

A word of warning: making a fluid transition between different hand patterns takes practice. So don't get discouraged if it takes a while before you get it right:

PATTERN 8-4

1	+	2	+	3	+	4	+	1	+	2	+	3	+	4	+
ᕦ	•	ᕦ	•	▲	•	O	O	ᕦ	O	ᕦ	•	▲	•	O	O
L	R	L	L	R	L	R	R	L	R	L	L	R	L	R	R

1	+	2	+	3	+	4	+	1	+	2	+	3	+	4	+
ᕦ	•	ᕦ	•	▲	•	O	O	ᕦ	O	ᕦ	•	▲	•	O	O
L	R	L	L	R	L	R	R	L	R	L	L	R	L	R	L

1	+	2	+	3	+	4	+	1	+	2	+	3	+	4	+
✳	•	•	▲	▲	•	O	O	✳	•	•	▲	▲	•	O	O
R	L	R	L	R	L	R	L	R	L	R	L	R	L	R	L

To go from alternating hands back to the paradiddle pattern, all you need to do is play the last note of the alternating-hands pattern with your *right* hand. That way you'll be set up to start the paradiddle pattern with your *left*. Again we've connected three charts below so you can see how this works. The first chart is the Kassa groove. The second chart is the same pattern except that it ends with the *right* hand. The third chart is the paradiddle pattern again:

1	+	2	+	3	+	4	+	1	+	2	+	3	+	4	+
✳	•	•	△	△	•	O	O	✳	•	•	△	△	•	O	O
R	L	R	L	R	L	R	L	R	L	R	L	R	L	R	L

1	+	2	+	3	+	4	+	1	+	2	+	3	+	4	+
✳	•	•	△	△	•	O	O	✳	•	•	△	△	•	O	O
R	L	R	L	R	L	R	L	R	L	R	L	R	L	R	R

1	+	2	+	3	+	4	+	1	+	2	+	3	+	4	+
◡	•	◡	•	△	•	O	O	◡	O	◡	•	△	•	O	O
L	R	L	L	R	L	R	R	L	R	L	L	R	L	R	R

Once you can make a smooth transition going either direction, try switching back and forth. Then try switching back and forth between the paradiddle pattern and any of the other alternating-hands patterns you've learned.

The next pattern is a hybrid. It's a complex dance but it's well worth the effort. The pattern starts with alternating hands. Then on 3 in the first measure it switches to a paradiddle that starts with the right hand. On 3 in the second measure it switches back to alternating hands. If you leave the left hand down after playing the heel and toe on 2 and the AND of 2 in the second measure it will function just like a drop and make the slap that follows crisper.

This is another pattern that works best with a little swing. If you find yourself doing the funky chicken while you play it, you'll know you're playing it correctly:

PATTERN 8-6 **PLAY-ALONG**

1	+	2	+	3	+	4	+	1	+	2	+	3	+	4	+
✱	•	•	◡̇	Δ	•	O	O	◡	O	◡	•	Δ	•	O	O
R	L	R	L	R	L	R	R	L	R	L	L	R	L	R	L

Paradiddle

PATTERN 8-6 (IN 4/4)

1	e	+	a	2	e	+	a	3	e	+	a	4	e	+	a
✱	•	•	◡̇	Δ	•	O	O	◡	O	◡	•	Δ	•	O	O
R	L	R	L	R	L	R	R	L	R	L	L	R	L	R	L

3/4 time

The easiest way to understand 3/4 time is to think of it as an abbreviated version of 4/4. Since we've been counting mainly in cut-time, let's take a moment to review 4/4.

In 4/4, each pulse is divided into four sixteenth notes, and there are four pulses to a measure:

1	e	+	a	2	e	+	a	3	e	+	a	4	e	+	a

In 3/4, each pulse is also divided into four sixteenth notes, but there are just *three* pulses to a measure:

1	e	+	a	2	e	+	a	3	e	+	a

Because there's an odd number of pulses in 3/4, there's technically no backbeat. But you can create a double backbeat feel by putting a slap on each second and third pulse. That's what you'll do in the first pattern:

PATTERN 9-1

1	e	+	a	2	e	+	a	3	e	+	a
✳	•	•	•	Δ	•	•	•	Δ	•	O	O
R	L	R	L	R	L	R	L	R	L	R	L

In the next pattern, instead of a slap on the third pulse there are slaps on both sides of it:

PATTERN 9-2

1	e	+	a	2	e	+	a	3	e	+	a
✱	•	•	•	Δ	•	•	Δ	•	Δ	O	O
R	L	R	L	R	L	R	L	R	L	R	L

The next pattern is the same as the last except we've added a tone on the AND of 1:

PATTERN 9-3

1	e	+	a	2	e	+	a	3	e	+	a
✱	•	O	•	Δ	•	•	Δ	•	Δ	O	O
R	L	R	L	R	L	R	L	R	L	R	L

The next pattern uses basses at the start to create a call and response feel:

PATTERN 9-4

1	e	+	a	2	e	+	a	3	e	+	a
✱	•	•	✱	✱	•	•	Δ	•	Δ	O	O
R	L	R	L	R	L	R	L	R	L	R	L

Now create a different feel by putting slaps on both sides of the *second* pulse and filling in all the beats that follow:

PATTERN 9-5

1	e	+	a	2	e	+	a	3	e	+	a
✱	•	•	Δ	•	Δ	O	O	Δ	Δ	O	O
R	L	R	L	R	L	R	L	R	L	R	L

The next pattern is the same as the last except we've replaced the slap on the beat after the third pulse with a touch:

PATTERN 9-6

1	e	+	a	2	e	+	a	3	e	+	a
✳	•	•	△	•	△	O	O	△	•	O	O
R	L	R	L	R	L	R	L	R	L	R	L

Now combine patterns 9-5 and 9-6 to create a longer phrase:

PATTERN 9-7   PLAY-ALONG

1	e	+	a	2	e	+	a	3	e	+	a
✳	•	•	△	•	△	O	O	△	•	O	O
R	L	R	L	R	L	R	L	R	L	R	L

1	e	+	a	2	e	+	a	3	e	+	a
✳	•	•	△	•	△	O	O	△	△	O	O
R	L	R	L	R	L	R	L	R	L	R	L

Songs in 3/4 are relatively uncommon in popular music. If you're looking for a great one to play along with, try the title track from Steely Dan's "Two Against Nature."

lesson

Slap on the backbeat in six

For those of us raised in the rock and pop world of four, the world of six is uncharted territory. By **six** we mean two measures of **6/8 time**, where there are 6 eighth notes to a measure and each eighth note gets one beat. The pulse falls on beats 1 and 4 in each measure, and each pulse is divided into three beats:

1	2	3	4	5	6	1	2	3	4	5	6

On each chart in six there are four pulses, just as there were on each chart in four. And since we've defined a backbeat as every second pulse, in six the backbeat falls on 4 in each measure.

Musical Time-Out: Counting in six

We could have counted patterns in six in a single measure of 12 eighth notes. This way of counting is called **12/8 time** and it looks like this:

1	+	a	2	+	a	3	+	a	4	+	a

Counting in 12/8 has the advantage of putting the pulse on each numbered beat. But we chose to chart in 6/8 for several reasons. We find it's easier to work with two short 6-beat measures than with one long 12-beat measure. We also like the counting system in 6/8 better because each beat gets its own number. Rhythms in 6/8 are also a lot easier to talk about than rhythms in 12/8. (You already know how we feel about referring to the "uh" of 4.)

If you're used to counting in 12/8 and don't want to change, that's fine. Just think of each two-measure chart as a single measure of 12/8 instead. This won't change the sound or the speed of the patterns. And to help you out, we've included a chart in 12/8 for at least one of the patterns in each lesson in six.

Start by playing the pulse in six with a bass on 1, a slap on the back-beat, and touches on all the empty beats. When you make a stroke on every beat in six with alternating hands, the pulse moves back and forth between your right hand and your left – basses in the right and slaps in the left. It will help to count out loud at first, accenting the pulse in your voice: "**1**, 2, 3, **4**, 5, 6." And don't forget to keep the pulse going somewhere in your body too:

PATTERN 10-1

1	2	3	4	5	6	1	2	3	4	5	6
✳	•	•	Δ	•	•	✳	•	•	Δ	•	•
R	L	R	L	R	L	R	L	R	L	R	L

PATTERN 10-1 (IN 12/8)

1	+	a	2	+	a	3	+	a	4	+	a
✳	•	•	Δ	•	•	✳	•	•	Δ	•	•
R	L	R	L	R	L	R	L	R	L	R	L

Grooves like this one and the variations that follow will fit with lots of songs in contemporary world music. If you're looking for songs to play along with, you can check out three of our favorite African artists: Salif Keita, Oumou Sangare, and Oliver Mtukudzi. If you're looking for something closer to home, try playing along with the old Beatles song "Norwegian Wood." This is the best way to get a feel for how patterns in six work.

Now let's move on to some variations of the original pattern. Start by adding two tones at the end of the second measure:

PATTERN 10-2

1	2	3	4	5	6	1	2	3	4	5	6
✳	•	•	Δ	•	•	✳	•	•	Δ	O	O
R	L	R	L	R	L	R	L	R	L	R	L

You can keep the pattern up in the air longer by replacing the bass on 1 in the second measure with a slap in the *right* hand. It's like you're tossing the slap back and forth between your hands:

PATTERN 10-3

1	2	3	4	5	6	1	2	3	4	5	6
✳	•	•	Δ	•	•	Δ	•	•	Δ	O	O
R	L	R	L	R	L	R	L	R	L	R	L

Another way to vary the original pattern is to thicken the groove with extra basses. Start by adding a bass in your right hand on 3 in the second measure. Listen to the CD on this one to make sure you're playing it correctly. If you're not careful, you may find yourself feeling the pattern in four instead of six:

PATTERN 10-4

1	2	3	4	5	6	1	2	3	4	5	6
✳	•	•	Δ	•	•	✳	•	✳	Δ	•	•
R	L	R	L	R	L	R	L	R	L	R	L

In the next pattern we've taken out the bass on 3 in the second measure, and added a bass on 6 in the second measure instead. To get your left hand ready to play this extra bass, start moving it forward immediately after it plays the slap on 4:

PATTERN 10-5

1	2	3	4	5	6	1	2	3	4	5	6
✳	•	•	Δ	•	•	✳	•	•	Δ	•	✳
R	L	R	L	R	L	R	L	R	L	R	L

The next pattern includes both the extra basses from the last two patterns – on 3 and 6 in the second measure:

PATTERN 10-6

1	2	3	4	5	6	1	2	3	4	5	6
✳	•	•	△	•	•	✳	•	✳	△	•	✳
R	L	R	L	R	L	R	L	R	L	R	L

Now let's go back to the original pattern again and start fresh by adding a bass in the right hand on 5 in the second measure.

PATTERN 10-7

1	2	3	4	5	6	1	2	3	4	5	6
✳	•	•	△	•	•	✳	•	•	△	✳	•
R	L	R	L	R	L	R	L	R	L	R	L

In the next pattern we've taken out the bass on 5 in the second measure, and added a bass on 6 in the first measure instead. To get your left hand ready to play this extra bass, start moving it forward immediately after it plays the slap on 4 (just as you did in pattern 10-5):

PATTERN 10-8

1	2	3	4	5	6	1	2	3	4	5	6
✳	•	•	△	•	✳	✳	•	•	△	•	•
R	L	R	L	R	L	R	L	R	L	R	L

The next pattern includes both of the extra basses from the last two patterns – on 6 in the first measure and 5 in the second. This one's a tongue twister, so take it slow at first. Once you get it, you won't want to stop. The play-along version is at the end of track 10 on the CD:

1	2	3	4	5	6	1	2	3	4	5	6
✳	•	•	△	•	✳	✳	•	•	△	✳	•
R	L	R	L	R	L	R	L	R	L	R	L

Another way to put a slap on the backbeat is to take the tumbao pattern you learned in four and swing it all the way to six. When you do that, the notes on the ANDS in four move to the beat before each pulse in six. The beat after each pulse in six remains empty. We've put a chart of the tumbao pattern in four above the same pattern swung to six so you can see the connection:

PATTERN 7-3

1	+	2	+	3	+	4	+
⌐	•	△	•	⌐	•	O	O
L	L	R	L	L	L	R	R

PATTERN 10-10

1	2	3	4	5	6	1	2	3	4	5	6
⌐		•	△		•	⌐		•	O		O
L		L	R		L	L		L	R		L

PATTERN 10-10 (IN 12/8)

1	+	a	2	+	a	3	+	a	4	+	a
⌐		•	△		•	⌐		•	O		O
L		L	R		L	L		L	R		L

This groove is often called a shuffle. It's used a lot in rock and blues, so you should have no trouble finding songs to play along with.

The 6/8 bell

We've saved some of our favorite grooves for last. They're based on a beautiful bell pattern found in music all over the world. It's called the 6/8 bell and it goes like this:

PATTERN 11-1

1	2	3	4	5	6	1	2	3	4	5	6
X		X		X	X		X		X		X

PATTERN 11-1 (IN 12/8)

1	+	a	2	+	a	3	+	a	4	+	a
X		X		X	X		X		X		X

This pattern is often used in African and Afro-Cuban ensembles as a timeline, like the clave pattern you learned in Lesson 4.

A good way to learn the 6/8 bell is to clap the pattern while you step the pulse. Before you try it, take a moment to study the relationship between the notes of the bell pattern and the pulse. In particular, notice that the bell pattern coincides with the pulse on 1 in the first measure and 4 in the second. On the CD, you'll hear how the bell pattern sounds with the pulse played on a shaker immediately following the bell pattern played alone:

PATTERN 11-1

1	2	3	4	5	6	1	2	3	4	5	6
X		X		X	X		X		X		X

Now count out loud and get the pulse going on 1 and 4 in your feet. Go slow at first. When you're ready, start clapping the 6/8 bell. If you can't clap the whole pattern all the way through, wade in gradually, adding a note or two at a time. Whatever you do, don't let this pattern

– or any pattern – intimidate you. If you take your time and take small enough steps, you can learn anything.

**Don't let any pattern intimidate you.
If you take your time and take small enough steps,
you can learn anything.**

Like the 6/8 bell pattern, the grooves based on it are challenging to play. So we're going to build our way up to them step by step. Start by playing basses on the pulse and tones on 5 and 6:

PATTERN 11-2

1	2	3	4	5	6	1	2	3	4	5	6
✳	•	•	✳	O	O	✳	•	•	✳	O	O
R	L	R	L	R	L	R	L	R	L	R	L

When you add a slap on 3, you're playing a djembe part from Tiriba, a rhythm from Guinea:

PATTERN 11-3

1	2	3	4	5	6	1	2	3	4	5	6
✳	•	△	✳	O	O	✳	•	△	✳	O	O
R	L	R	L	R	L	R	L	R	L	R	L

You can play a similar pattern – with a slap on 3 and tones on 5 and 6 – with your hands in a "T" formation. The pattern is called tumbao in six, and it's the same as tumbao in four with a heel-toe taken out of each measure. We've put a chart of a single measure of tumbao in four above a single measure of tumbao in six so you can see the connection:

PATTERN 7-3 TUMBAO IN FOUR

1	+	2	+	3	+	4	+
⊃	•	△	•	⊃	•	O	O
L	L	R	L	L	L	R	R

PATTERN 11-4 TUMBAO IN SIX

1	2	3	4	5	6
⊃	•	△	•	O	O
L	L	R	L	R	R

Here's a full two-measure chart of tumbao in six:

PATTERN 11-4

1	2	3	4	5	6	1	2	3	4	5	6
⊃	•	△	•	O	O	⊃	•	△	•	O	O
L	L	R	L	R	R	L	L	R	L	R	R

Like its cousin in four, tumbao in six is a versatile and popular groove. When in doubt, check it out.

Now you're going to leave the "T" formation and go back to pattern 11-3 and build from there. The next pattern is the same as pattern 11-3 except that the slap in each measure falls on 2 instead of 3. It's easy to get turned around on this one, so make sure you keep feeling the bass in your right hand as 1. It may help to say "one" every time you play it:

1	2	3	4	5	6	1	2	3	4	5	6
✳	△	•	✳	O	O	✳	△	•	✳	O	O
R	L	R	L	R	L	R	L	R	L	R	L

The next pattern combines a measure of pattern 11-3 with a measure of pattern 11-5 to create a groove that tracks most of the notes of the 6/8 bell. We've shaded the notes of the 6/8 bell on the count row so you can see the connection. Notice that you play the slap in the first measure with your right hand and the slap in the second with your left:

PATTERN 11-6 $\quad$ PLAY-ALONG

1	2	3	4	5	6	1	2	3	4	5	6
✳	•	△	✳	O	O	✳	△	•	✳	O	O
R	L	R	L	R	L	R	L	R	L	R	L

PATTERN 11-6 (IN 12/8)

1	+	a	2	+	a	3	+	a	4	+	a
✳	•	△	✳	O	O	✳	△	•	✳	O	O
R	L	R	L	R	L	R	L	R	L	R	L

The next pattern is the same as the last except we've taken out the bass on 4 in the first measure:

PATTERN 11-7

1	2	3	4	5	6	1	2	3	4	5	6
✳	•	△	•	O	O	✳	△	•	✳	O	O
R	L	R	L	R	L	R	L	R	L	R	L

In the next pattern, we've taken out the two tones at the end of the second measure. Instead, there's a bass in the left hand on 6 in the second measure, matching the note at the end of the bell pattern:

PATTERN 11-8

1	2	3	4	5	6	1	2	3	4	5	6
✳	•	Δ	•	O	O	✳	Δ	•	✳	•	✳
R	L	R	L	R	L	R	L	R	L	R	L

We've shaded the boxes of the 6/8 bell on the next chart so you can see that when you take out the bass on 1 in the second measure, the pattern tracks the bell pattern note for note:

PATTERN 11-9

1	2	3	4	5	6	1	2	3	4	5	6
✳	•	Δ	•	O	O	•	Δ	•	✳	•	✳
R	L	R	L	R	L	R	L	R	L	R	L

The next pattern is the same as the last except for the last three notes:

PATTERN 11-10

1	2	3	4	5	6	1	2	3	4	5	6
✳	•	Δ	•	O	O	•	Δ	•	Δ	O	O
R	L	R	L	R	L	R	L	R	L	R	L

Now combine pattern 11-10 and 11-9 to create a longer phrase. Notice that the two patterns are identical until 4 in the second measure of each:

1	2	3	4	5	6	1	2	3	4	5	6
✳	•	△	•	O	O	•	△	•	△	O	O
R	L	R	L	R	L	R	L	R	L	R	L

1	2	3	4	5	6	1	2	3	4	5	6
✳	•	△	•	O	O	•	△	•	✳	•	✳
R	L	R	L	R	L	R	L	R	L	R	L

Musical Time-Out: The 6/8 bell

We've always agreed that if our house were on fire and we could only take one rhythm with us, the 6/8 bell pattern would definitely be it. Then a few years ago, Ken Dalluge, a percussionist from Santa Cruz, amazed us by pointing out the correspondence between the structure of this universal rhythmic pattern and the structure of the major scale.

This correspondence is easiest to understand if you think of the boxes on one of our charts in six as the keys on a piano, with the box on ONE as middle C. The notes of the bell pattern line up perfectly with the white keys on the piano. Where there's an empty box on the chart, there's a black key on the piano. This correspondence is either one of the most amazing coincidences in the history of the planet or it reflects a mysterious underlying unity between tonality and rhythm.

CHAPTER 5

Glossary

backbeats: every second pulse in a pattern with two or four pulses. 21

beats: subdivisions of a pulse. 17

clave: an instrument used in Afro-Cuban music consisting of two cylindrical pieces of wood struck together and the timelines played on those instruments. 40

closed slap: a slap where you momentarily grip the drumhead with your fingers. 24

cut-time: a way of counting in four with two pulses to a measure and each pulse divided into four eighth notes. 17

fill: a rhythmic bridge between repetitions of a pattern or sections of a song. 28

four: a pattern is in four if it can be notated on a chart with four pulses and four subdivisions to each pulse. 17

4/4 time: a way of counting in four with four quarter-note pulses to a measure and each quarter note divided into four sixteenth notes. 17

funk swing feel: a style of playing in four created by playing the notes on the ANDS slightly closer to the numbered beats (counting in cut-time). 48

offbeats: the beats that fall between pulses (except upbeats). 31

ONE: the first beat in the first measure. 47

open slap: a slap where you bounce your fingers off the drumhead immediately. 24

paradiddle: a drumset rudiment with the hand pattern RLRR or LRLL. 64

pulse: the underlying metronomic rhythm people feel in their bodies when music is played. 16

six: a pattern is in six if it can be notated on a chart with four pulses and three subdivisions to each pulse. 72

6/8 time: a way of counting in six with six eighth notes to a measure. 72

straight-eighth feel: a feel created by dividing a pulse into only two beats. 34

timelines: asymmetrical repeating rhythmic patterns used as reference rhythms in African and Afro-Cuban music. 40

12/8 time: a way of counting in six with four pulses to a measure and three eighth- note subdivisions to each pulse. 72

upbeats: the beats exactly midway between pulses. 32

1	+	2	+	3	+	4	+	1	+	2	+	3	+	4	+

1	+	2	+	3	+	4	+	1	+	2	+	3	+	4	+

1	+	2	+	3	+	4	+	1	+	2	+	3	+	4	+

1	+	2	+	3	+	4	+	1	+	2	+	3	+	4	+

1	+	2	+	3	+	4	+	1	+	2	+	3	+	4	+

1	e	+	a	**2**	e	+	a	**3**	e	+	a	**4**	e	+	a

1	e	+	a	**2**	e	+	a	**3**	e	+	a	**4**	e	+	a

1	e	+	a	**2**	e	+	a	**3**	e	+	a	**4**	e	+	a

1	e	+	a	**2**	e	+	a	**3**	e	+	a	**4**	e	+	a

1	e	+	a	**2**	e	+	a	**3**	e	+	a	**4**	e	+	a

1	+	2	+	3	+	4	+	1	+	2	+	3	+	4	+

1	+	2	+	3	+	4	+	1	+	2	+	3	+	4	+

1	+	2	+	3	+	4	+	1	+	2	+	3	+	4	+

1	+	2	+	3	+	4	+	1	+	2	+	3	+	4	+

1	+	2	+	3	+	4	+	1	+	2	+	3	+	4	+

1	e	+	a	2	e	+	a	3	e	+	a

1	e	+	a	2	e	+	a	3	e	+	a

1	e	+	a	2	e	+	a	3	e	+	a

1	e	+	a	2	e	+	a	3	e	+	a

1	e	+	a	2	e	+	a	3	e	+	a

1	2	3	4	5	6	1	2	3	4	5	6

1	2	3	4	5	6	1	2	3	4	5	6

1	2	3	4	5	6	1	2	3	4	5	6

1	2	3	4	5	6	1	2	3	4	5	6

1	2	3	4	5	6	1	2	3	4	5	6

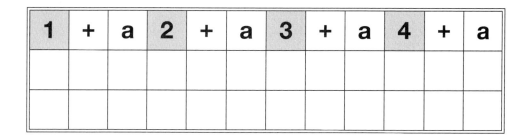

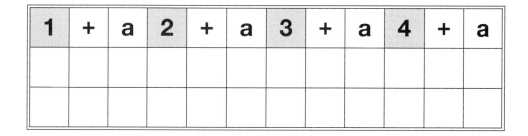

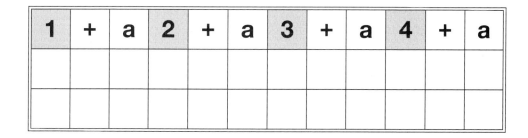

1	+	a	2	+	a	3	+	a	4	+	a

1	+	a	2	+	a	3	+	a	4	+	a

Also available from Dancing Hands Music

$24.95

DRUM MAGAZINE
Best
Percussion
Method
Book
2000 READERS' POLL

Conga Drumming
A Beginner's Guide to Playing with Time

BY ALAN DWORSKY AND BETSY SANSBY

This 160-page book with CD is a complete, step-by-step course on conga drumming. It teaches families of drum parts for several authentic Afro-Caribbean rhythms, including rumba, bomba, calypso, conga, and bembe. We use a simple charting system and the same friendly teaching style as HIP GROOVES FOR HAND DRUMS. Life-like illustrations show you the proper technique for each stroke. And the CD that's included contains a sample recording of each of the 175 drum parts taught in the book as well as examples of how the parts sound together.

"**Fantastic!**" – RHYTHM MAGAZINE

"**There is no other source** for this kind of information that is as simply and sensibly explained, and contains such a wealth of rhythms. CONGA DRUMMING welcomes rather than intimidates beginners. Dig into this book and in a very short time you will be playing well. Bravo and muchas gracias Alan and Betsy!"
– DRUM MAGAZINE

"**The best book of its kind.**"
– ARTHUR HULL

How to Play Djembe
West African Rhythms for Beginners

BY ALAN DWORSKY AND BETSY SANSBY

"**A superb work ... it makes learning easy and fun, and Joh Camara's playing on the play-along CD is a joy to hear.**" – PROFESSOR MICHAEL WILLIAMS, DEPARTMENT OF MUSIC, WINTHROP UNIVERSITY

This book has all the best features of HIP GROOVES, including the same easy-to-read charts and life-like illustrations. In addition to learning proper djembe technique, you'll learn interlocking parts for seven popular West African rhythms. The CD that comes with the book was recorded by Joh Camara, a master drummer from Mali, and each track is at least five minutes long so you'll have plenty of time to play along.

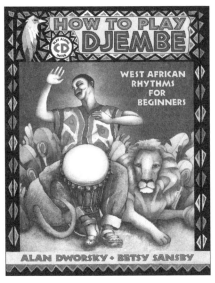

$24.95

93

Secrets of the Hand
Soloing Strategies for Hand Drummers

BY ALAN DWORSKY AND BETSY SANSBY

This book is for hand drummers who want to play complex solos using simple sequences of hand strokes. Whether you play conga or djembe, the practical hand-pattern strategies explained here will help you get the most out of your hands with the least amount of effort. And whether you want to solo in a traditional African or Afro-Cuban ensemble, in a drum circle, in a band, or in your living room along with your favorite CDs, SECRETS OF THE HAND will help you take your playing to the next level.

$24.95
CD with sample of every pattern
in **Secrets of the Hand**
now available at dancinghands.com

World-Beat & Funk Grooves
Playing a Drumset the Easy Way

BY ALAN DWORSKY AND BETSY SANSBY

"It doesn't get any more accessible than this"
— DRUM MAGAZINE

This book takes patterns like the ones in HIP GROOVES FOR HAND DRUMS and applies them to the drumset. It uses an ingenious method that makes complex rhythms magically emerge out of simple sequences of body movements. Within days you'll be playing patterns that usually take months to master. It comes with 2 CDs: one contains samples of every pattern in the book, the other is a timelines CD you can play along with while you practice.

$24.95
Free sample lesson at
dancinghands.com

Jaguar at Half Moon Lake

BY DANCING HANDS

"A luminous debut." — NEW MUSIC SERIES REVIEW

This CD of original music features Indie-award winning Dean Magraw on acoustic guitar and several world percussionists, including master drummer Coster Massamba on djembe. You can hear excerpts from JAGUAR on tracks 12–16 of the CD that comes with HIP GROOVES FOR HAND DRUMS.

$13.95

Learn to Solo on Djembe or Conga
A Step-By-Step Course

WITH ALAN DWORSKY

This series is for advanced hand drummers who want to learn to solo in a systematic way using an audio-visual approach. It's designed to prepare you to solo in a traditional ensemble, a drum circle, or a band.

Each lesson is available in two formats: as a video with printed charts or as a CD with an instructional booklet.

LESSON 1: The Power of Pairs
LESSON 2: The Rippled 8 and the Illusion of Speed
LESSON 3: The Perfect Lick – The Rippled 6
LESSON 4: The Funky Offbeat Path
LESSON 5: Hip Deep in Six
LESSON 6: Getting Off the Grid with Quarter-Note Triplets

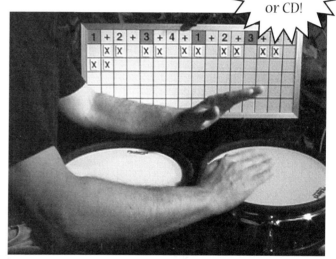

"An ingenious method for understanding the mystery of how to solo – hidden from most hand drummers until now!"
– GARY MEITROTT, FOUNDER AND DIRECTOR OF DRUM JOURNEYS OF EARTH

Videos are $19.95 each and are also available in European PAL format

You can see sample clips at dancinghands.com

CD/booklets are $14.95 each

$19.95

Slap Happy
How to Play World-Beat Rhythms With Just Your Body and a Buddy

BY ALAN DWORSKY AND BETSY SANSBY

SLAP HAPPY is a fun, funky way for kids of all ages to learn about rhythm. We've taken drum rhythms from Africa and the Caribbean (including some of the grooves from HIP GROOVES) and turned them into body rhythms you can step, clap, and slap with a buddy. You can do SLAP HAPPY in pairs or in groups, indoors or out, at home or at school. If you're a parent, it's a great way to do something fun and educational with your kids. If you're a music teacher, you can use SLAP HAPPY to give your students a hands-on experience of world rhythms without having to buy any instruments. And you can hear how every pattern sounds on the slap-along CD that comes with the book.

96